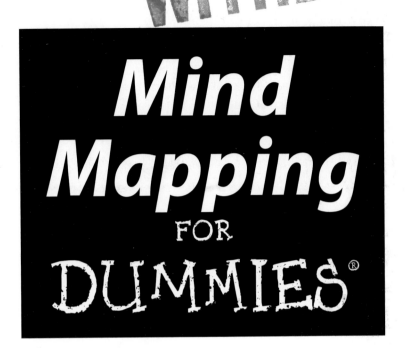

Mind Mapping

FOR

DUMMIES®

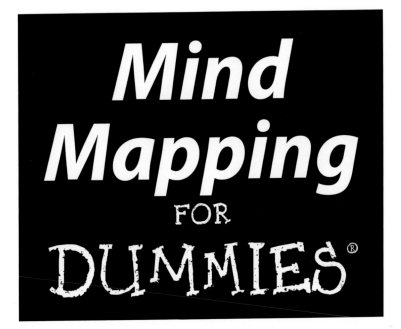

by Florian Rustler

Foreword by Tony Buzan

A John Wiley and Sons, Ltd, Publication

Mind Mapping For Dummies®

Published by
John Wiley & Sons, Ltd
The Atrium
Southern Gate
Chichester
West Sussex
PO19 8SQ
England

Email (for orders and customer service enquires): cs-books@wiley.co.uk

Visit our home page on www.wiley.com

For general information on our other products and services, please contact our Customer Care Department within the U.S. at 877-762-2974, outside the U.S. at 317-572-3993, or fax 317-572-4002.

For technical support, please visit www.wiley.com/techsupport.

Wiley also publishes its books in a variety of electronic formats and by print-on-demand. Some content that appears in standard print versions of this book may not be available in other formats. For more information about Wiley products, visit us at www.wiley.com.

British Library Cataloguing in Publication Data: A catalogue record for this book is available from the British Library

ISBN: 978-1-119-96915-0 (pbk), 978-1-119-94375-4 (ebk), 978-1-119-94376-1 (ebk), 978-1-119-94377-8 (ebk)

Printed and bound in China by Toppan Leefung

10 9 8 7 6 5 4 3 2 1

WILEY

About the Author

Florian Rustler is an innovation coach working at international level and the founder of *creaffective*.

As a process moderator he presents strategy and innovation workshops in German, English and Mandarin Chinese to help his clients produce new solutions quickly; for example, when developing new products and services.

As a tutor he teaches organisations the processes and techniques of creative problem solving and assists them with generating an innovation culture.

He learned Mind Mapping while still at school. A teacher introduced the technique in just ten minutes during class but then took it no further. However, Florian didn't let these ten minutes go to waste. He got hold of Tony Buzan's book on Mind Mapping, the only one available at the time, and subsequently applied the technique. He later qualified as a Mind Mapping tutor and since then has given hundreds of Mind Mapping classes and published an online Mind Mapping course.

You can find out more about him at: www.creaffective.de.

Publisher's Acknowledgements

We're proud of this book; please send us your comments through our Dummies online registration form located at www.dummies.com/register/.

Some of the people who helped bring this book to market include the following:

Commissioning, Editorial and Media Development

Project Editor: Rachael Chilvers

Commissioning Editor: Kerry Laundon

Assistant Editor: Ben Kemble

Technical Editor: Gillian Burn

Translation Services: Absolute Translations Ltd

Proofreader: Jamie Brind

Production Manager: Daniel Mersey

Publisher: David Palmer

Cover Photo: © iStock / mattjeacock

Cartoons: Rich Tennant (www.the5thwave.com)

Composition Services

Project Coordinator: Kristie Rees

Layout and Graphics: Lavonne Roberts, Laura Westhuis

Proofreader: Rebecca Denoncour

Indexer: Claudia Bourbeau

Publishing and Editorial for Consumer Dummies

Kathleen Nebenhaus, Vice President and Executive Publisher

Kristin Ferguson-Wagstaffe, Product Development Director

Ensley Eikenburg, Associate Publisher, Travel

Kelly Regan, Editorial Director, Travel

Publishing for Technology Dummies

Andy Cummings, Vice President and Publisher

Composition Services

Debbie Stailey, Director of Composition Services

Contents at a Glance

Table of Contents

Foreword

*M*ind Mapping For Dummies is an apt idea, as Mind Mapping is something we already know how to do – we do it constantly without even realising it!

Mind Mapping replicates the way our brains think and the way we absorb information. When we think of any idea, our mind instantly starts connecting this to other images, thoughts and concepts. So why do we force ourselves to make notes, plan and create in a way that our brain doesn't like?

When I was at university, struggling to study with the mass of lined notes I had made, Mind Mapping helped me to make sense of the information, reduce my notes and remember more. Now it is doing the same for millions of people around the world, helping them to be more productive, creative and efficient in their everyday lives. Join them, and start using the full potential of your mind every day.

With this guide, Florian has created a comprehensive resource on Mind Mapping, which will be of great use to those wanting a step-by-step guide to using this powerful tool, also known as the 'Swiss Army Knife' of the brain! This book shows you how to Mind Map, what to avoid and gives you the information you need to navigate the jungle of Mind Mapping software out there.

You find out how versatile the Mind Map really is, and how you can apply this technique to plan, study, manage projects, solve problems and brainstorm.

Enjoy exploring the potential of your amazing mind!

Tony Buzan

Introduction

Many people have heard of Mind Mapping at least once or twice – and presumably you too, since you're holding this book in your hand! Or you saw the front cover with the Mind Map and found it somehow familiar. Mind Mapping has now become so widespread and well-known that the term has entered English usage.

What is Mind Mapping? Mind Mapping is a visual technique for structuring and organising thoughts and ideas.

If this sounds all rather general and wide-ranging, then you can also use Mind Mapping in a general and wide-ranging fashion, whether you generate Mind Maps with a pen and paper or with special Mind Mapping software.

Many people have heard of Mind Mapping but don't really know what it's all about. Or perhaps you're one of those people who know what Mind Mapping is and have tried working with it, perhaps with Mind Mapping software installed at work. Somehow it didn't work out and the method failed to live up to its promise. I want to change that with this book, for Mind Mapping is a very powerful method that can be of great assistance in many aspects of life. Whether you're a complete novice or already have some experience of Mind Mapping, this book is bound to be of benefit to you.

About This Book

Mind Mapping For Dummies equips you in five parts with everything you need to successfully apply the Mind Mapping techniques. As a qualified Mind Mapping tutor I have introduced Mind Mapping to thousands of people in seminars and so have a good idea of how the technique can help and what difficulties people usually encounter when learning it. The composition of this book is based on the structure of one such seminar.

So, I start with the principles of Mind Mapping and then take you through various and increasingly complex areas of the technique. You discover how to use both pen and paper and Mind Mapping software in this book. The method is the same however you generate maps.

Conventions Used in This Book

If this isn't your first book in the *For Dummies* series, you'll recognise many aspects from other volumes in the series. I use the following conventions:

- ✔ *Italics* are used for words or concepts
- ✔ The action part of numbered steps are in **bold**.

Foolish Assumptions

There are many reasons for using this book and I assume that one or more of the following descriptions applies to you:

- ✔ You're frequently confronted at home or at work with the challenge of structuring and organising information.
- ✔ You're looking for a clear and simple way of doing so.
- ✔ You want to find a method that enables you to work in a more efficient and structured manner.
- ✔ You want to learn Mind Mapping or to extend the knowledge you already have of this technique.

Mind Mapping is a technique. To be able to use it effectively, you have to acquire the right skills. Just like swimming, driving or learning a musical instrument, it requires some practice. In theory, I could explain to you in ten minutes what driving a car, swimming or playing the guitar involves. If you'd never driven a car before you'd still be unable to do so after ten minutes of theory. It's similar with Mind Mapping. To acquire the necessary skills you have to do one thing in particular: you need to use Mind Mapping.

Hence my basic assumption about you, the reader, is as follows: you're prepared to do the exercises in this book and are aware that this isn't just a book to be read on the train. I encourage you to actively generate Mind Maps as you read this book.

How This Book Is Organised

Mind Mapping For Dummies contains five parts. Depending on how intensively you have already worked with Mind Maps and what you want to use Mind Maps for, some chapters may be more important to you than others. Apart from Part I which I encourage you to read, there's no fixed order. Part IV covers advanced strategies for using Mind Maps. To understand and master these, you need Parts II and III.

Part 1: Mind Mapping: The Swiss Army Knife for the Brain

In this part you find out why it's so important to visualise thoughts and information and why you shouldn't merely write them down in lists or as running text. When you've explored the basic advantages of visualising information and how they can be applied, I explain the fundamental rules for generating Mind Maps. Chapter 3 is central to all subsequent chapters in the book. After you've assimilated these rules, you may be wondering why you need them. Why Mind Mapping works as it does and how Mind Mapping has come about I explain in the last chapter of Part I.

Part II: Traditional Mind Mapping in Practice

Part II introduces the technique's main areas of application, such as structuring and organising information, using Mind Mapping to make notes from books and in meetings, and preparing talks and lectures. Part II covers Mind Maps which are generated with a pen and paper. Moreover, all the applications presented in Part II are also possible with software.

Part III: Mind Mapping Software

Part III is devoted to Mind Mapping software. With Mind Mapping software you can combine the possibilities of Mind Map visualisations with the advantages of computing. I first guide you through the impenetrable forest of Mind Mapping programs and then present two such programs, *MindManager* and *iMindMap* in detail.

Part IV: Advanced Strategies for Mind Mapping

In Part IV I introduce you to advanced applications of Mind Mapping. In addition to Mind Mapping techniques for efficient reading of textbooks, you learn more about using Mind Maps for exam preparation. You also learn how to use Mind Mapping for project and knowledge management.

Many people regard Mind Mapping as a creative technique. This is too limited, but Mind Mapping can still play a role in creative processes. In the last chapter of Part IV I show you just how this works.

Part V: The Part of Tens

Part V provides a number of tips and tricks in the form of top-ten lists to help you apply Mind Mapping effectively to your everyday work. I also provide details of a number of websites on the subject.

Icons Used in This Book

Symbols with the following meanings appear alongside the text:

Remember these little gems of wisdom.

Here you can find practical instructions on how to make Mind Mapping easier for you.

This symbol highlights special features, of Mind-Mapping software for example.

Beware! Here you need to exercise caution or query your assumptions.

Where to Go from Here

This book is arranged in five parts in modular fashion. If you think that you don't need a particular application of Mind Mapping and aren't curious about what you can learn in the section, you can omit the section concerned.

If, however, you decide at some point to return to a chapter you previously omitted, you can do so easily. I recommend that you first read Part I which introduces the principles of Mind Mapping on which subsequent sections build. Even if you think that you're familiar with the basics of Mind Mapping, I strongly recommend that you read Chapter 3 on generating Mind Maps. In my classes I often find that students who think they already know how to work with Mind Mapping still learn something new in this section.

If you're now ready and willing to learn Mind Mapping, then let's get started. Before you do, you need to have the following items to hand:

🖊 White unlined sheets of A4 or, even better, A3 paper

🖊 Some coloured pens

Have fun!

Part I
Mind Mapping: The Swiss Army Knife for the Brain

When Leroy's brainstorming session deteriorated to stick figures, he decided to give Mind Mapping a try.

In this part . . .

A lot of people know about Mind Mapping as a concept but without really understanding what actually lies behind the technique.

In this part I set out the principles and background for your subsequent work with Mind Mapping. You learn how important it is to visualise information rather than just writing it out as text. You discover Mind Mapping rules and gain an insight into the many areas in which it is used. Lastly I explain why Mind Mapping works so well.

Chapter 1

Introducing Mind Mapping

In This Chapter

▶ What characterises a Mind Map

▶ How to create your first Mind Map

▶ What you can use Mind Maps for

*W*ould you like to know how to create a Mind Map? Before we get started, I first want to give you an idea of what a Mind Map actually is and how many different opportunities there are for using Mind Mapping. I can assure you: you'll soon find this technique absolutely indispensable.

Presenting Information Visually

If you flip through the many Mind Maps depicted in this book you'll notice that they look more like pictures than text. Mind Maps are a bit like a tree looked at from above, with its branches radiating out in all directions from the trunk. You'll also notice that Mind Maps do contain actual words but that these are always reduced to mere keywords.

A Mind Map, for example the Mind Map specimen in this chapter, can contain the same information as the continuous text in the chapter itself. The main difference is that in a Mind Map content is not presented in lines and rows as in continuous text but is actually visualised. In addition to keywords, visualisation involves a sequence of graphic elements such as:

- ✔ Colours
- ✔ Symbols
- ✔ Pictures
- ✔ Spatial arrangement of branches

The second main difference is that a Mind Map is an individual, personalised map, which reveals the thoughts of its creator. This means that Mind Maps are not automatically self-explanatory, since no two people would create exactly the same thought structure. Nevertheless, Mind Maps can also be understood by other people; for instance, when you've read the content of the book or already know something about the topic.

You can use the specimen Mind Maps in each chapter in a number of ways, for example, by taking a quick look at them just before reading a chapter without understanding everything in them or after reading a chapter as a quick recap of its content. This is also helpful if you pick up the book again after a break and want to recall the material.

Give it a try!

Mind Mapping is a technique that you can learn from, work with and put into practice. Let's start with an exercise. The exercise gives you your first taste of setting up a Mind Map and introduces you to Mind Mapping procedures.

To master Mind Mapping properly, work through the exercises described in the book. Just reading it through without doing the exercises won't enable you to apply Mind Mapping successfully. Mind Mapping is a technique and the best way to learn it is by putting it into practice. As you start writing and creating your mind map you activate your 'muscle memory', meaning that you *remember* the information more than by just reading it. The exercises and instructions in this book help you to do this as effectively as possible.

Please have the following to hand:

- ✔ A sheet of A4 or, even better, A3 paper.
- ✔ A pen with a fine point, for example a biro.

And now let's get started:

- ✔ Write the word 'Success' in the middle of your sheet of paper (see Figure 1-1).
- ✔ Draw a sort of frame or cloud around the word (later on you'll learn about leaving the central word 'open', increasing creativity).
- ✔ To the central concept attach six branches that are long enough for a word to be written on them. Remember to keep the branches quite short to start with – you can always make them longer afterwards.

   Mind Mapping doesn't prescribe how many main branches a theme should have. That depends entirely on the theme concerned. In this exercise I stipulate the number of main branches: there should be six.

Figure 1-1:
Six main branches around the central theme.

✔ Take a couple of minutes to consider what you associate with the notion 'Success' and what concepts or ideas occur to you in this connection. Write each of your concepts in the form of one (!) keyword on one of the branches of the Mind Map.

✔ For each word consider whether and how you could express the concept in visual form. Then write or draw them beside the keyword on the branch concerned. Don't worry, artistic quality is not an issue here!

After five minutes your first Mind Map may look something like Figure 1-2.

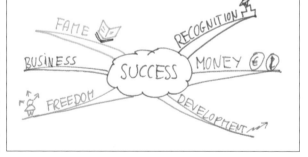

Figure 1-2:
Six associations for the theme of Success.

If you now compare your six associations with my associations you'll probably see that you associate completely different concepts from mine with the theme of Success. That's quite normal, as everybody has different experiences and a different background and hence also different associations.

Even if you and a colleague draw up a Mind Map of a very specific professional theme quite independently of each other you'll be surprised at just how different your Mind Maps look.

Taking the Mind Map a stage further

Use a further ten minutes or so to take your Success Mind Map a stage further by drawing sub-branches from each main branch and adding greater detail. There's no limit on how many sub-branches you can add to each main branch. Just put them wherever further associations arise and extend the Mind Map accordingly.

You can:

✔ Add sub-branches at as many levels as you like

✔ Attach as many sub-branches to the same level as you like

✔ Jump to and from individual themes within your Mind Map

In Chapter 4 I explain just how people think. One feature of our brain is that it thinks by association and by leaps and bounds. You can make use of these characteristics with Mind Mapping by extending your thoughts at a point in the Mind Map where they're best suited.

Now start the exercise and come back to the book after about ten minutes.

Figure 1-3 contains my own example for this exercise.

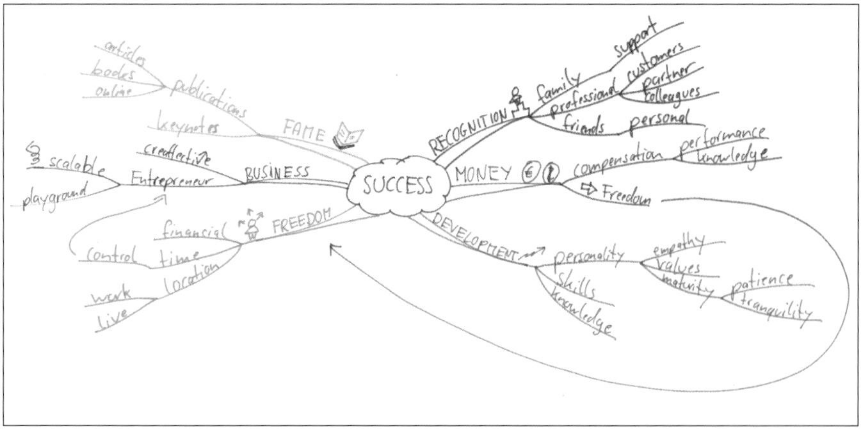

Figure 1-3:
Mind Map
taken a
stage
further.

Free association or strict logic?

When drawing in the sub-branches for each of your six concepts you'll make associations which at first sight have no direct connection with the central theme of Success. Figure 1-3 depicts the concept 'Business' as a main branch on my Mind Map. With this concept of 'Business' I associate, among other things, the concept of 'Entrepreneurship' meaning perhaps that I'd like to found a number of companies in my lifetime. From the concept of 'Entrepreneurship' I arrive at the concept of 'Playground'. In my specific case I'd like to found a number of small companies as a playground for my ideas!

In my Mind Mapping seminars I sometimes meet people who weigh up each new concept on the Mind Map and ask whether it really has a strictly logical connection with the theme of the Map. In our case I might wonder whether the concept 'Playground' is really logically connected with my theme of 'Success'. When drawing up the Mind Map in this exercise, try not to worry whether each word can really be traced back logically to the central idea. Otherwise you'll only restrict yourself and, at worst, write down nothing at all. Allow your thoughts and associations free rein.

A little reflection please

Now that you've finished this exercise I've the following questions for you:

- ✔ This first exercise on 'Success' took you a total of 15 minutes. In your view, what are the differences with 'normal' messages which you simply write down?

- ✔ If I'd asked you to express your thoughts on the theme of Success instead of producing a Mind Map in just 15 minutes, would the number of thoughts and their depth have been similar?

In my seminars I often get the following feedback when I ask these two questions:

- ✔ The Mind Mapping process provides a flow of associations and so it's much easier to add new thoughts.

- ✔ In this way significantly more ideas are generated than in normal messages.

- ✔ The structure of the Mind Map allows you to add new thoughts at every point without having to squeeze them in somewhere.

- ✔ The practice of working with key concepts and branches enables you to penetrate a theme much more quickly and deeply.

- ✔ The spatial arrangement of branches displays connections and links between themes which could not be identified in linear representations.

A Simple Technique with Many Applications

Mind Mapping involves a couple of easily assimilated ground rules. With this set of rules you can apply Mind Mapping to many situations, wherever information has to be structured and organised. This could also be as simple as a compiling 'shopping list' (see Figure 1-4). But you'll usually use Mind Mapping in more complex areas.

Frequent applications of Mind Mapping are:

- ✔ Manuscripts and 'cribs' for lectures and presentations
- ✔ Notes from texts and books
- ✔ Notes from talks, presentations and discussions
- ✔ Project management
- ✔ Knowledge management
- ✔ Exam preparation

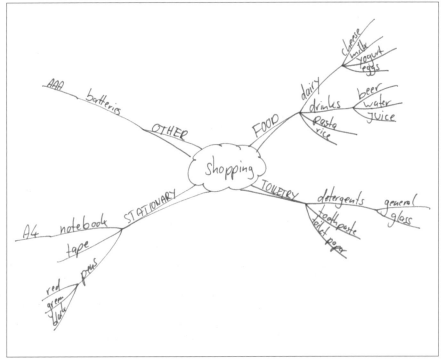

Figure 1-4:
Shopping list with Mind Mapping.

'Cribs' for lectures and presentations

All important content required for a lecture or planned presentation can be contained in a Mind Map readily and clearly for you to access. The visual form of the Mind Map gives you an overview of your material so that you can speak to your audience freely, naturally and effectively.

Of course it's also possible to supplement a lecture with additional visualisations like well-known PowerPoint presentations. With Mind Mapping software you can also present a lecture to an audience visually as a Mind Map.

In Chapter 5 I demonstrate in detail how you can use this technique to draft notes for talks and lectures.

Taking notes from texts and books

Mind Mapping allows you to summarise the most important content of many text and book pages in one or more Mind Maps.

It's clear, particularly in the case of notes from books, that Mind Maps are devised mainly for the person who made the Mind Map concerned and are not usually comprehensible to other people. For a person who's read a book and, while reading, made notes from it using Mind Mapping, the Mind Map's the key to recalling the book's content.

How to make notes from texts and books is the subject of Chapter 6 where you'll learn and practise this procedure.

Taking notes from presentations and discussions

This application of Mind Mapping's based on a similar principle. With Mind Mapping you can glean important information from discussions and presentations easily and, above all, very quickly. The essential thing about Mind Mapping – and its great strength – is that you can organise content thematically and not necessarily in the chronological order of a discussion or presentation. This means that, instead of writing down all the information sequentially as you would when taking ordinary notes, you can add new information flexibly to the Mind Map at any time in a way that makes thematic sense. This is particularly useful in unstructured discussions and presentations. In Chapter 7 you'll learn how effective notes can be taken in lectures and discussions and practise this technique.

Assistance with study

During both my undergraduate and post-graduate study I organised my notes and book excerpts in the form of Mind Maps, sometimes with pen and paper and sometimes with the software available at the time. All these Mind Maps are scanned and stored on my computer and are accessible to me in digital format. Even years after completing my studies it can often happen that I'd like to look up a topic that I covered at that time and clarify an issue relating to it. In this way Mind Maps that I made then are still extremely useful to me today. Without having to search through the details of texts and pages of notes I can conjure up all the required information in just a few minutes. In Chapter 16 I describe in detail how this is done.

Project management

When it's a matter of planning and organising projects, Mind Mapping can help you to gain a quick and easy overview of the issues and recognise connections among the individual elements of your project.

Mind Mapping software's particularly helpful with project management. In this way you can:

- ✔ Make changes flexibly to a Mind Map.
- ✔ Convert the Mind Map to other file formats.
- ✔ Use additional functions of the program that are relevant to project management, such as the inclusion of time scheduling and personal details.
- ✔ Display a timeline as a GANTT diagram.
- ✔ Integrate digital information and create digital links from your Mind Map.

You could also use Mind Mapping to present project management on a single page. Best of all, you've visualised the content of the project and so simplified your task.

You can find detail on how to deploy Mind Mapping in project management in Chapter 14.

Knowledge management

As has already been shown, you can summarise the content of books, discussions and lectures with Mind Maps. With Mind Mapping software you can link together these different areas of knowledge to develop your own form of knowledge management. By linking several Mind Maps together you can navigate around entire fields of knowledge and call up content at any time. Chapter 15 book demonstrates with several examples how you can manage knowledge with Mind Mapping.

Pen and Paper or Computer?

One day when I was talking to a company on the phone, the lady there told me that, if possible, her employes ought to learn Mind Mapping by computer. By 2005 computers were everywhere. Quite right too. And yet, even in 2012, despite the long hours they spend at their computer, most people still use a pen a paper to write with. Indeed, it's hard to imagine a child learning how to write on a computer without first practising by hand. It's a similar situation with Mind Mapping.

The essential thing is the Mind Mapping technique itself, irrespective of whether it's tackled with a pen and paper or computer. It's very important to master the thought processes and procedures associated with Mind Mapping. At the beginning this is often easier with a pen and paper than with a computer.

You can then decide which situations are best suited to either method of Mind Map preparation. In fact, you'll need both methods.

Pen and paper are often preferable when:

- ✔ It's impractical or undesirable to use a computer, for example, in many kinds of meeting.
- ✔ The computer doesn't provide the flexibility you get with a pen and paper.
- ✔ Drawing a Mind Map with pen and paper helps you to assimilate content better, for example, when preparing for exams. This method helps as you initiate your 'muscle memory' as mentioned previously.

On the other hand, computers and software offer possibilities that far exceed what can be done with pen and paper, so working on a computer may be particularly suited to project and knowledge management. Whenever the content of a Mind Map needs to be altered often or you need to work on content together with other people, you are better off with a computer.

Mind Mapping software provides the possibility of:

- Generating different views of a Mind Map (condensing and expanding).
- Filtering Mind Maps according to specific criteria.
- Linking Mind Maps with other documents.
- Presenting Mind Maps electronically.
- Converting Mind Maps to other data formats and processing them further.
- Searching Mind Maps by using keywords.

Lastly, with software there are no problems of space and you can update and alter the content as often as you like.

You can find out more about the differences between Mind Mapping with pen and paper and Mind Mapping software in Chapter 8. In Chapter 9 I provide you with an overview of the many different software programs. In Chapters 10 and 11 you get to know both the Mindjet MindManager and iMindMap programs in detail.

I devote the whole of Part III to the topic of Mind Mapping software.

Revising Mind Maps

If you produce Mind Maps with a pen and paper you'll often encounter situations where you'd like to revise your Mind Map because the following problems have arisen:

- You've made a mistake and had to cross it out several times and rewrite. Now the Mind Map doesn't look as nice as you'd like it to.
- After you've drawn a Mind Map you realise that you'd like to organise it differently so that it provides an overview of the entire topic.
- You've encountered difficulties of space when drawing a Mind map and had to divide a theme into several main branches.

Don't regard the production of another version of a Mind Map as additional work or wasted time but consider it as a chance to understand a theme better and rework it more precisely. Revising a Mind Map helps you to get to grips with a theme more closely.

Advanced Strategies Using Mind Mapping

When you have a basic grounding in Mind Mapping you can then combine the technique with other processes to increase your work efficiency.

In Chapter 12 you learn more about special reading strategies that quickly enable you to read works of non-fiction very efficiently and extract their essential content. This involves a combination of skim-reading techniques and Mind Mapping. The way in which Mind Maps are produced enables you to read as little as possible but as much as you need.

Mind Mapping can also be used effectively in group situations aimed at developing new ideas and solutions. Despite what's often written, Mind Mapping's not appropriate for joint brainstorming sessions. The technique's not best suited to this. Mind Mapping proves useful, however, when generated ideas need to be organised and structured so they can be taken further. I demonstrate in Chapter 16 how this can be done.

In fact, Mind Mapping is a technique with applications in many different areas. When you reach the end of this book you'll be familiar with all the areas mentioned above and be able to decide what you can use the technique for.

Chapter 2
Visualising Information

· ·

In This Chapter

▶ How and why visualisation can help you

▶ Categorising visualisation methods

▶ The background and origins of Mind Mapping

· ·

*W*hy should you bother to visualise information? After all, you can just write it out as text. In this chapter I want to show you that visualising information has many advantages that aren't shared by text on its own.

How and Why Visualisation Can Help You

In his book *Brain Rules* the American neurobiologist John Medina suggests that humans are visual creatures and can assimilate and store visual information far more effectively than, say, acoustic information:

> 'We are incredibly good at recording images. If you hear some information, then three days later you will remember only 10% of it. If you add a picture to it, then 65% will be retrievable'.

You're probably familiar with the saying 'a picture paints a thousand words'. Not all sayings are correct but this one has a lot of truth to it and has even been confirmed scientifically.

In specialist jargon there's an expression 'Pictorial Superiority Effect', which means that visual stimuli take precedence over other sensory stimuli in the brain. In *Brain Rules* John Medina states that the more visual the information is the more easily it's absorbed and retained. The reason for this is evolutionary: in our distant past we received much of our essential information in the form of moving images and so our brains are particularly good at recognising, storing and recalling visual information.

Text as a form of visual information

By now it's probably occurred to you that text is also a form of visualisation, as it's something you can see. It's true that text is also processed via the visual system. However, text is less effective than images for recognising, understanding and retaining information. The reason is that our brains see words as myriad tiny images. As far as the human brain is concerned, there are no words but just images that have to be interpreted as words. As each word uses the same brain resources as a picture, an image uses a lot less brain processing time than text containing the same ideas.

Reducing complexity and presenting information in a different way

The more often you can reduce chunks of text and replace them with a visualisation, the better it is for your brain. By presenting information in a different way and displaying it visually you enable your brain to:

✔ Assimilate information more quickly

✔ Retain content more effectively

✔ Recall content more rapidly

Most of the information you'll be exposed to in future will also be as text, since it's still the easiest way of communicating impersonally. But text consists of rows and rows of similar symbols and so is incapable of depicting connections on its own.

Two examples

I'd like to show you two examples which illustrate effective visualisation. They are effective because they provide associations and insights that are not possible with description alone. The objects in the figures quickly allow the viewer to notice associations.

Figure 2-1 (taken from: www.aattc.org.au/Times%20December%20 1999W.pdf) shows a rail timetable from 1985 in the People's Republic of China. Edward Tufte describes it in his book *Envisioning Information* as a clever multifunctional combination of a map and data table. The diagram is a mixture of route map and index. The numbers in the figure refer to pages of the 200-page timetable catalogue so the reader can look up precise departure times. It also provides a complete geographical overview of all destinations and estimates of distance.

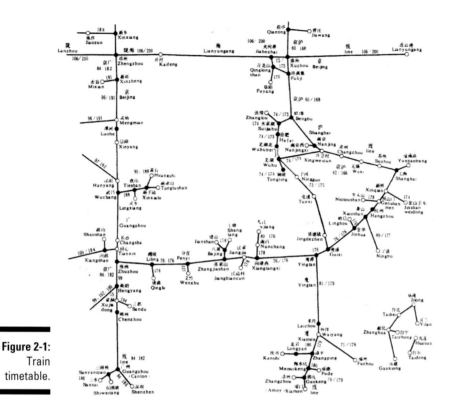

Figure 2-1:
Train
timetable.

However, sometimes visualisation also needs additional clarification in the form of text, at least when the visualisation has not been produced by you yourself.

Figure 2-2 displays an 'innovation portfolio', a method allowing innovative projects to be evaluated from market and business perspectives. The diagram enables you to see at a glance the differences between projects and makes it easier to decide which projects should be followed up.

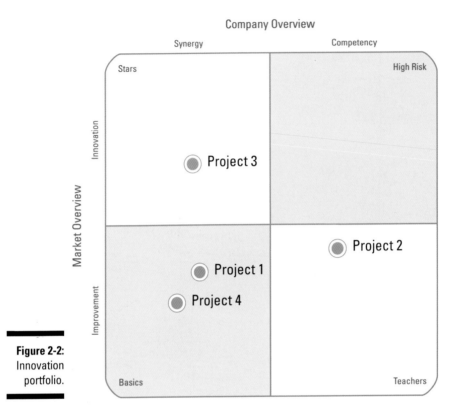

Figure 2-2:
Innovation
portfolio.

Visualising Information as a Core Skill

You are aware of it every day: the plethora of information and its complexity are increasing all the time. And yet you have to deal with it somehow. This makes the ability to visualise information, thereby allowing the brain to assimilate it easily, comprehensively and efficiently, a core skill for modern brain workers.

Linguistic training (learning the alphabet) is an essential element of our educational system. Linguistic competence denotes the ability to make sense of written or verbal language. Some researchers believe that not just linguistic competence but also *visual literacy* needs to be taught. Visual literacy is the ability to assess, apply and generate visual representations.

Of course, you can present information graphically in any way you like. But there is already a host of visualisation methods, which have been continually improved over many years, to help you.

What science has to say

Scientists Ralph Lengler and Martin J. Eppler of the University of Lugano define visualisation methods as follows:

> *'A systematic, rule-based, external, permanent and graphic representation which presents information in a way which promotes and further develops insight and understanding or communicates experience.'*

Lengler and Eppler started the *Visual Literacy* project and developed a periodic system (see Figure 2-3) that provides an overview of the different kinds of visualisation and their methods.

Figure 2-3 displays the periodic system of visualisation methods (on the internet at www.visual-literacy.org). By clicking on each of the elements displayed in the periodic system at the website you can call up examples and further information.

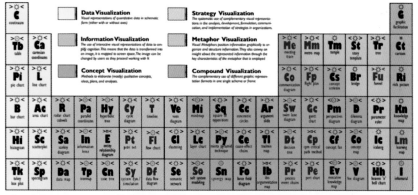

Figure 2-3: Periodic system of visualisation methods.

Lengler and Eppler distinguish between the following kinds of visualisation methods:

✔ **Methods for visualising quantitative data:** For example, a pie chart, which may already be familiar to you from Excel files.

✔ **Methods for visualising information:** Information is more than just data. Data contain no hint as to their use. Information is typically connected with a particular situation and possesses context.

One example of an information visualisation technique is the so-called pie model (see Figure 2-4, taken from `www.visual-literacy.org/periodic_table/periodic_table.html#`).

✔ **Methods for visualising concepts:** These methods extend the ways of visualising information by containing further clarification.

Mind Maps, the focus of this book, are an example of this.

✔ **Methods for visualising strategies:** A portfolio diagram is an example of this kind of visualisation technique (see Figure 2-2).

✔ **Methods for visualising metaphors:** For example, the graphic representation of a bridge, tree or iceberg metaphor.

✔ **Combined visualisation methods:** This involves combining several visualisation methods in a single image.

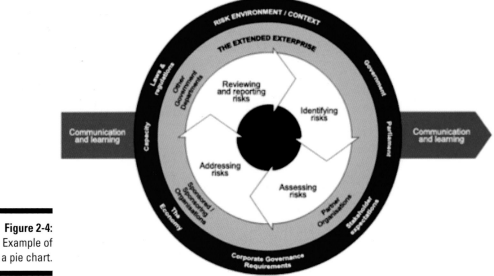

Figure 2-4:
Example of a pie chart.

Going back in time: The origins of Mind Maps

Anyone familiar with Mind Maps has come across the name Tony Buzan (he also wrote the foreword of this book). Buzan is considered to be the inventor of Mind Mapping. He was a former science reporter and formalized the Mind Mapping technique in the 1970s on the basis of research into the brain and learning current at that time. A major source of inspiration was the 'Split Brain' research of Roger Sperry. This research was based on epilepsy sufferers whose *corpus callosum*, the connection between the brain's hemispheres, had been cut.

This showed that different mental functions are assigned to various parts of the brain's hemispheres. The research led to a recognition that the brain has several ways of organising and processing information. For example, in addition to processes based on speech and logic there's also graphic and spatial localisation.

Sperry and his research team have never asserted, as has been wrongly ascribed to them, that the brain can be divided into two separate halves that act independently of each other. The notion that the brain can be separated into a logical–analytical left half and a chaotic–creative right half and that, as a consequence, different types of people such as 'left-brainers' and 'right-brainers' exist, is a

myth which unfortunately is still purveyed by some authors, despite the fact that this thesis was abandoned by the scientific community 15 years ago. However, it's still cogently argued and, in addition, the brain-half myth is apparently borne out in practice, which explains why it still has currency today.

The analysis of records of extraordinary people who are renowned for their accomplishments also encouraged the development of Mind Maps. It's striking that such people very often use visual representations and drawings to establish their thoughts and ideas.

In the 1970s Tony Buzan was also lecturing as an educational psychologist on the use of the brain and realised he could improve the effect of his lectures by encouraging his students to use their brains differently. He developed an operations manual of the brain which became part of a successful BBC series called *Use Your Head*.

Using this and other background information, Buzan developed and formalised the visual technique of Mind Mapping, which is the subject of this book. Mind Mapping is a graphic technique based on a few rules that allows you to visualise, structure and organise a multiplicity of information in a meaningful way.

The visualisation method used for Mind Mapping

This book focuses on the visualisation method used for Mind Mapping. Lengler and Eppler attribute the following properties to Mind Maps:

> ✔ Mind Maps are a means of visualising concepts. This is more than the mere presentation of information, since additional clarification is provided.

✔ Mind Maps are used to visualise knowledge structures (as opposed to processes).

✔ Mind Maps provide both an overview and the detail of a theme.

✔ Mind Maps are useful for developing and displaying a multiplicity of ideas and information.

Chapter 3

Generating Mind Maps

● ●

In This Chapter

▶ Understanding the meaning of basic rules

▶ Using branches to structure all information

▶ Working with keywords to establish core information

▶ Using graphic elements to exploit the possibilities of Mind Mapping

▶ Developing your own style step by step

● ●

*M*ind Maps are discrete thought maps – hence the name of the technique. If you generate and use Mind Maps correctly you can structure, organise and visualise nearly all kinds of information effectively. A Mind Map helps you to form your ideas, associations and impressions in ways that are:

✔ Sensible to you.

✔ Easy to memorise.

✔ Individual and easily recalled to mind.

These features of Mind Maps mean, for example, that you can now fit the content of an hour-long meeting into a single page. This not only saves space but also time, since, when you look at your Mind Map again, the process used to generate it and your memories of the meeting are recalled to mind. What you wrote is immediately accessible again. The best thing is that it works not only in the short term but for years afterwards.

Whether it's the content of a lecture you have to give, the notes of a meeting or a whole book that you need to summarise, Mind Maps can contain all the required information on one or more pages and present it clearly and effectively.

In this chapter I describe how you can generate Mind Maps correctly, allowing you to work effectively with the technique and to benefit from its advantages. Just like the slogan of an old TV commercial, the history of Mind Maps is 'a history full of misunderstandings'. Many 'visualisations' promoted as Mind Maps are nothing of the sort, at least not in the sense of the technique presented in this book.

The Basic Rules: Helping You to Use Mind Mapping Effectively

The Mind Mapping technique offers you a lot of individual freedom in how you design your maps. Indeed, it's the individuality of Mind Maps that makes them so versatile.

Adapt the technique to your own style and working procedure to get the best out of Mind Mapping.

Just like football, Mind Mapping has a number of basic rules. In sport, basic rules make a successful game possible. It's just the same with the basic rules of Mind Mapping. These few rules enable you to work really successfully with the technique. Soon you'll no longer even think about the rules, as they'll be second nature.

Branches – it's all connected

Figure 3-1 contains an example of a Mind Map and presents a typical structure.

What are the differences between a Mind Map and an ordinary drawing? Some differences are immediately apparent. Unlike the traditional way of pre-senting information in writing, for example on this page, a Mind Map doesn't start at the top left and end at the bottom right. A Mind Map always begins in the middle of your page or screen with the so-called *central idea*. The central idea contains the topic of the Mind Map and is rather like the title of a book. All further information in a Mind Map is connected to the central idea in the form of branches. You develop your Mind Map on plain paper so you're not constrained by lines. Ideally position your paper sideways (landscape), to provide greater wider vision and space for being creative.

Main and secondary branches

Two kinds of branches can be distinguished:

- **Main branches:** These are connected directly to the central idea and contain the principal themes of a Mind Map. The main branches are rather like the chapters of a book.

- **Sub-branches:** These connect to the main branches on as many layers as you like and contain the subsidiary and detailed information of the Mind Map.

In a Mind Map each and every piece of information is written on branches or sub-branches. A Mind Map leaves no content floating around somewhere in the ether. Everything, whether words or pictures, is written on branches.

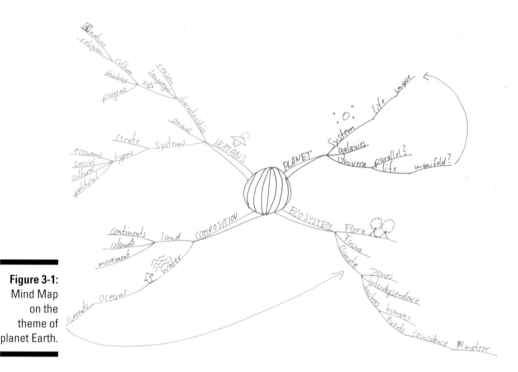

Figure 3-1:
Mind Map
on the
theme of
planet Earth.

The length of each branch or sub-branch is important. Aim to keep the length of the line you write on as short as possible, ideally it should be the same as the length of the word.

Wavy or curvy lines (sometimes called organic, flowing lines) are also preferable to straight lines as they're more creative and help to act as a memory tool.

Using branches correctly

I'll quickly give you a couple of important tips on using branches:

✔ Take care that the branches always connect to each other. If you add a sub-branch to an existing branch, then they should always be joined directly together. Branches grow out of each other, just as in a tree. There must be no gaps between the end of a branch and the beginning of a sub-branch. The branches connect directly to each other (see Figure 3-2).

If you add a sub-branch to a branch, place it at the end of the branch concerned (see Figure 3-2, keyword 'beside'). If a branch already has so many sub-branches that there's not enough space left, you can also connect sub-branches to the underside of a branch (see Figure 3-2, keyword 'underside').

Avoid connecting a branch across a word or right in front of it. This spoils the Mind Map's visual clarity and hierarchy. In the case of complex Mind Maps in particular, this may mean that you can no longer navigate around the map.

✔ You can include as many sub-levels as you wish. There's no restriction on these. However, in my experience five or six levels are usually enough.

✔ An individual branch can contain as many sub-branches as you like. There's no limit on this either. Just how many branches you attach depends entirely on the topic of the Mind Map concerned. Just one sub-branch is also possible. Unless the Mind Map is subdivided into parts, '1.1' on the map must always come immediately before '1.2'.

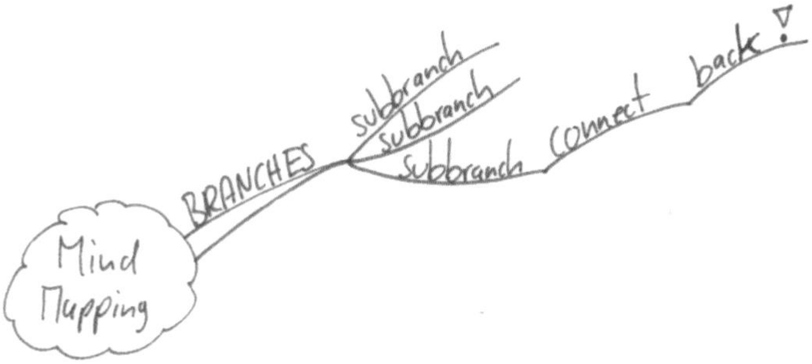

Figure 3-2:
Branches
connected
together.

A Mind Map grows like a tree from the trunk outwards. Every branch can divide as often as you like. The important thing is that two branches should never rejoin further out, that is, terminate in another branch. That doesn't happen on a real tree either. Why? Because it'd prevent you from extending the theme and hence your Mind Map, when this is necessary.

Keywords instead of phrases

Another important aspect that for some people is unfamiliar and new is the so-called keyword rule.

Each branch of a Mind Map contains just one keyword. Yes, that's right! Mind Mapping tries to to get by with just one keyword per branch. In Mind Mapping, instead of writing 'good friends' on a branch you write just 'friends'. The adjective 'good' then appears on a sub-branch attached to the word 'friends' (see Figure 3-3).

Perhaps you're wondering what use this rule is. I'll show you in the following example.

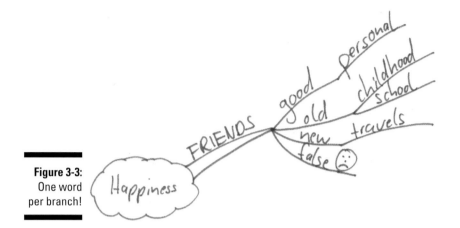

Figure 3-3:
One word
per branch!

One word per branch

What occurs to you when you read the two words 'lilac cow'. If you have a sweet tooth I bet the notions 'chocolate' and 'Milka' definitely come to mind. But most other people wouldn't necessarily make these connections with the words 'lilac cow'.

What associations come to mind if I say just one word, the word 'cow'? Now your thoughts may fly off in all directions and notions such as 'milk', 'farm', 'pasture', 'mountains', 'meadow', 'faithful', 'stupid' and, of course, 'lilac' might occur to you.

Take another example of two words: 'green and black'. Again, chocolate lovers may think of the connection with a certain chocolate brand. If each word was written separately, you open up your creativity to more possibilities: green grass, green vegetables, green paint, green traffic lights and so on.

Freedom of thought in all directions

The main difference between the above examples is that in the first instance (the two words 'lilac cow'), your thinking is directed firmly in a particular direction. You quickly arrive at Milka chocolate. However, as soon as I use just one word, your thoughts can literally take off in all directions. It's precisely this flexibility and freedom to extend a Mind Map at any time that the keyword rule provides.

Details of a keyword are written on the sub-branches of an existing branch. Of course, you can add detailed information to any word, but in Mind Mapping it's always written on sub-branches.

Figure 3-3 clarifies the principle at work with the example of the branch 'friends'. Moreover, by using just one word it's possible to insert further aspects of the theme as sub-branches, such as 'good friends', 'old friends' and 'false friends'. Writing just the word 'friends' on the branch means that you can write each of the other three aspects ('good', 'old' and 'false') on sub-branches. Logically, it'd make no sense to place the two words 'good friends' on one branch and then the word 'false' on a sub-branch. This extension of the theme would already be excluded by including the two words 'good friends' together.

Hence, the use of just one keyword per branch plays a number of important roles in Mind Mapping:

✔ The Mind Map remains clear and uncluttered.

✔ Thinking can proceed in any direction.

✔ The theme of a branch can be extended flexibly at any time.

✔ Further associations are stimulated.

The exception proves the rule

All rules have exceptions and this is also the case with this Mind-Mapping rule.

In two situations it's sensible to depart from this rule:

✔ **Personal names:** If you want to write the name of a person, organisation or product in your Mind Map, then it's placed on one branch, even if the name consists of several words, because it's a single unit.

✔ **Quotations:** For example, if you read a text and it's important to transcribe the precise wording of something on your map, then this can be written as a quotation on a single branch. You should mark it as a quotation, for example, by using speech marks.

Even though there are exceptions to the rule, always try to use single words and not interpret everything to be written on the Mind Map as a quotation. Otherwise, the advantages created by using single words are lost. Using keywords alone ensures that a Mind Map remains clear and uncluttered and a lot of information can be packed into it.

Using Mind-Mapping software and the *text memo* or *notes* function means that whole texts can be embedded within a keyword and recalled at will. This allows you to insert just one keyword but, at the same time, add further information. There's more on this in Chapters 10 and 11.

A Picture Says More Than a Thousand Words

Mind Mapping operates with a number of graphic elements. These elements are not just additional clutter but an essential part of the technique and contribute to its effectiveness.

Mind Mapping operates with the following graphic elements:

- ✔ Colours
- ✔ Symbols
- ✔ Pictures
- ✔ Boxes
- ✔ Connecting arrows

I now have a closer look at these elements and how they're used.

Colours – not just pretty to look at

If you generate Mind Maps with a pen and paper, your basic kit should include a couple of different coloured pens. Drawing Mind Maps with several colours can have a number of objectives:

- ✔ **Distinguishing the main branches from each other:** This is the principal use of colours. Each main branch and all its sub-branches are drawn and written in one colour. This helps with quick visual differentiation of themes and also makes the Mind Map more varied.

- ✔ **Highlighting particular meanings with different colours:** In many situations it's sensible and possible to associate a colour with a particular meaning which the colour stands for in the Mind Map. Thus, when you read your map you can identify at a glance the various aspects of a theme by the colours used.

  - You're using Mind Maps to take the minutes of a meeting in your company. Two groups, marketing and R&D, with different opinions on a subject, take part in this meeting. Now, for example, you can use the colour blue for marketing and green for R&D. The arguments of each group can then be added in the relevant places by using the right colours.

  - You're using Mind Maps to take notes as you read a textbook. You reserve a particular colour for your own thoughts and ideas and one for your objections and counter-arguments. You add your own thoughts at the relevant places in the map by using these particular colours. This means that, when you read through the Mind Map later on, it's obvious at a glance which parts were taken from the book and which bits represent your own thoughts.

Your personal set of symbols

In Mind Mapping, symbols are small graphics like the familiar icons in computer programs. Symbols have exactly the same function as icons on a computer. Using symbols means that you can quickly and easily add further content to a Mind Map visually. Because of their visual nature, symbols stand out from written text and are quickly and easily recognisable. So, symbols not only allow you to pack more meaning into a Mind Map but they also make the map quicker and easier to read. Symbols can be utilised in two ways:

✔ Symbols are drawn under, over or beside the word on a branch and so include additional meaning.

✔ Symbols stand alone on a branch in place of a keyword.

The important thing is that the symbols used should be meaningful to you, the creator of the Mind Map, and you can identify and easily recognise them. The symbols don't have to be comprehensible to everybody. A Mind Map is first and foremost a chart of your own thoughts. Therefore, it's essential that the symbols used should mean something to you personally.

Figure 3-4 demonstrates how symbols can be used in a Mind Map.

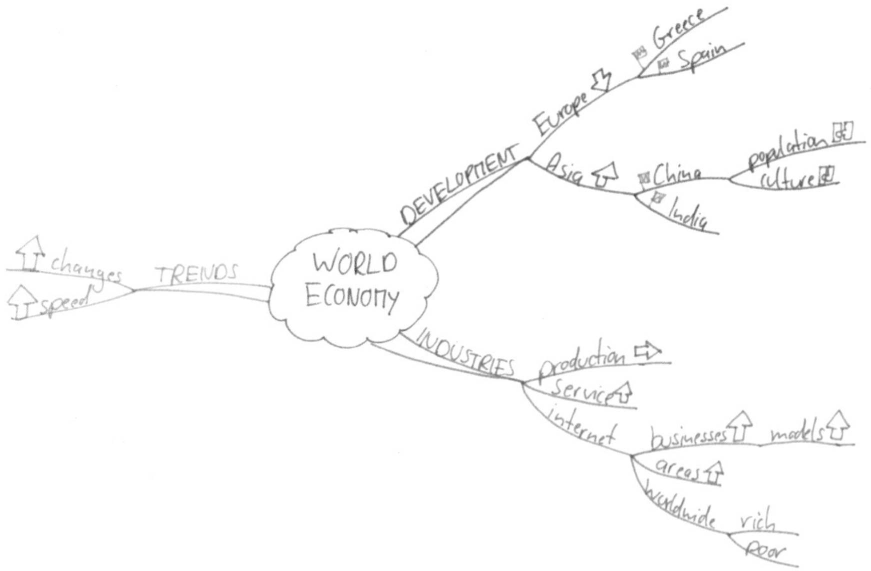

Figure 3-4:
Mind Map
with
symbols.

Figure 3-5 summarises the meaning of the symbols most frequently used by me.

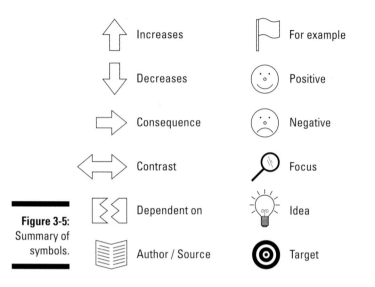

Symbols are useful if you want to express frequently used content and concepts graphically instead of always writing them out.

Gradually build up a personal set of symbols that are meaningful and useful for you. In my experience, after a couple of weeks of using Mind Maps your set will contain around 10 to 15 symbols. Over time you'll notice whether you use a particular symbol for a frequently used piece of content.

When developing symbols, you may be inspired by computer programs and especially by the Mind-Mapping programs in the accompanying book-DVD. The programs contain a large number of symbols which can also be used when drawing Mind Maps with a pen and paper.

To make the use of symbols more specific, I suggest some of my own personal symbols. The graphics are displayed in Figure 3-5:

- ✔ **Smileys:** I frequently want to indicate that something is good or positive. I personally use a laughing face for this and add it to a keyword on the branch. The opposite is also possible of course. If I want to mark something as negative or bad I then insert a sad face.

- ✔ **Arrow symbols:** Different kinds of arrows are also frequently used. To me, an arrow pointing upwards means that something is increasing and one pointing downwards that something is decreasing. A horizontal arrow symbolises a consequence or an outcome.

- **For example:** I personally use the expression *for example* a lot. I have devised my own symbol for this: a small flag. Whenever I see this flag I know that the keyword is an example of something that I've written on the branch.

- **Dependent on:** A sort of broken square to me means *dependent on*. It's often the case that I need such causal connections. For example, I read a text about stress that explains to me what factors stress depends on. I then put stress on a main branch and write the factors mentioned in the text on sub-branches. My 'dependent on' symbol is then written next to each factor. So, when I read it through later I'm immediately aware that a causal connection is involved.

- **Target:** The notion *target* often appears in my work, especially when I use Mind Maps to make notes in meetings. Instead of the words I merely write the symbol. Here too, when the Mind Map is reread the symbol catches my eye and helps me to assimilate the content more quickly.

- **Idea:** A light bulb as a symbol for an idea or notion is widespread and understood by many people. In my Mind Maps I sometimes use the light-bulb symbol in addition to a special colour to make a topic clear. This is particularly effective when I use Mind Mapping to structure the thoughts of others, for example when reading a book or minuting a meeting.

Boxes and clouds – highlighting what's important

Many people are used to underlining important points when reading texts or highlighting them with a marker pen. Of course, you can also use highlighters to mark individual branches when generating Mind Maps.

Another possibility with Mind Mapping is to include boxes and cloud symbols.

As Figure 3-4 shows, clouds can be deployed in several ways in Mind Mapping:

- You can emphasise a branch that seems especially important to you.

- By drawing in a cloud outline you can highlight a branch and all its sub-branches to give special emphasis to a whole thematic complex.

- You can also box in a branch and all its sub-branches. The role of the cloud is no longer to highlight something particularly important but to separate the individual main themes of a Mind Map even more clearly from each other.

It's a matter of personal style just how you use cloud outlines. I recommend that you use them sparingly to highlight only those aspects that are really important and to make them visible at a glance.

Making arrow connections quite clear

When working with Mind Maps it'll soon occur to you that branches in different parts of your Mind Map are thematically connected with each other. It can often happen that one and the same keyword crops up at different places in the map.

In my seminars I'm often asked whether it's a 'problem' if a particular word appears at several different places in a Mind Map. This isn't a problem, on the contrary: interesting information is frequently gleaned when a key concept crops up several times in different parts of a Mind Map.

In such instances it can be helpful to highlight the connection between two branches. You can insert connecting arrows to achieve this outcome in Mind Mapping.

In principle, you can draw in as many connecting arrows as you like. However, try not to overdo this and obscure the Mind Map with too much clutter and so lose the added value imparted by connecting arrows.

Figure 3-1 shows some examples of connecting arrows.

If you wish to join together two branches that are far apart from each other within a Mind Map, it's better to draw the connecting arrows around the edge of the map and not straight across the middle. This is a shorter route but it'll detract from the Mind Map's legibility.

Developing your own style

Mind Maps work so well because, among other things, they can be designed in a highly individual way; the greater the individuality of a Mind Map, the greater its recognition value for the author. Every Mind Map is a key that precisely fits the lock of the author's thoughts. Therefore, try to find your own style that's both suited and makes visual sense to you.

Mind-Mapping rules are very general and leave you a lot of space in which to develop your own style. Your personal style may be expressed, for example, by:

- ✔ The shape of branches
- ✔ The thickness of branches
- ✔ The use of graphic elements

Mind-Mapping rules provide a framework which ensures that the technique is effective and helpful for you. There's a lot of leeway for you inside this framework. Use it!

Chapter 4

Why Mind Mapping Works

. . . .

In This Chapter

▶ Understanding how people assimilate and process information

▶ Learning why pictures are important to us

▶ Knowing how we think

▶ Mind Maps as a brain-friendly technique

▶ When Mind Maps aren't the right method

. . . .

*T*ony Buzan, who developed Mind Mapping as I present it in this book, calls the technique the 'Swiss army knife for the brain'. Just like the famous Swiss army knife, a Mind Map is very easy to use and yet at the same time is very versatile. Using it, you can visualise, structure and organise almost any kind of information.

Moreover, Mind Mapping is not only simple and versatile but also brain friendly. What do I mean by that? The way in which Mind Maps are prepared and how they operate is naturally suited to the functioning of the human brain. Mind Mapping was developed in the 1970s on the basis of the latest findings (at the time) in the field of learning and memory. Discoveries of aspects of human thought processes influenced the development of Mind-Mapping rules. The upshot of this is that most Mind-Mapping users describe the technique as follows:

✔ Quick and easy to implement

✔ Easily memorised

✔ Quickly recalled

✔ Supports the generation of new thoughts and other notions

Mind Mapping is a tool that's easy and intuitive to use and helps us with our natural thought processes and information processing.

This is achieved because Mind Mapping is orientated towards the natural processes in our brains and takes the following aspects into account:

- There are many different ways in which we process and store information.
- Visual information plays a central role in our brains.
- We think by leaps and bounds and by association.
- We are especially good at memorising basic key concepts but quite poor at retaining a lot of detail.

These aspects are examined in greater detail below and then used to show how they're incorporated in the Mind-Mapping technique and why this makes Mind Mapping a very powerful, brain-friendly tool.

Different Routes to Information

Imagine that you have to take notes in a meeting or need to draw up a plan for a project. In both cases you have to process and present information.

The following elements play an important role in this:

- **Logic:** How you arrange the information. You organise it into aspects that are logical to you.
- **Rules:** The way in which you set out information follow rules that make sense to you. For example, in this book there are many models showing how information is structured. You'll probably have already noticed that I work a good deal with item lists in which information is presented.
- **Use of words:** Language plays a central role in assimilating and processing information and also in communicating and expressing information to other people. You assimilate the information in this book mainly by reading my text.
- **Use of numbers:** Another important way of processing and storing content involves numbers. They're used not only in counting and calculating but are also relevant when, for example, a sequence of things has to be expressed.

These aspects certainly come into play when you process and present information. Many books and texts are based on these elements alone. However, our brains also perceive other aspects, even if they don't occur in many books and texts:

- **Pictures:** Whether mental or real, pictures play a central role in our brains. In the next section I examine this aspect more closely.
- **Colours:** Different colours help us to distinguish between objects and to derive meaning from them. Colours often stand for a specific concept and are quickly perceived as such. Traffic lights are a good example of this.

✔ **Places:** The spatial arrangement of objects also contains information which we assimilate and use. For example, the principle of spatial organisation is utilised in many memorisation techniques. Articles we wish to memorise are associated with different parts of the body or are arranged mentally within a familiar room or along a familiar stretch of road. We can then return to these places in our minds and recall the information located there. This book uses the same principle by marking symbols with a particular meaning in the left-hand margin of the text concerned.

Pictures: Unique and unforgettable

Visual information plays a central role in our brains. In recent years this realisation has also become noticeable in many areas of our everyday lives, perhaps as a result of technical innovations. Examples are:

✔ Modern editions of school textbooks include significantly more illustrations and graphic elements than a few years ago.

✔ Newspapers and magazines are less inclined to present their content as blocks of text but rather as pictures and visualisations.

✔ More and more lecturers are using pictures and graphics to support their verbal content.

To return again to the example of talks and lectures: Figures 4-1 and 4-2 show two PowerPoint slides, both of which are supposed to express the same thing.

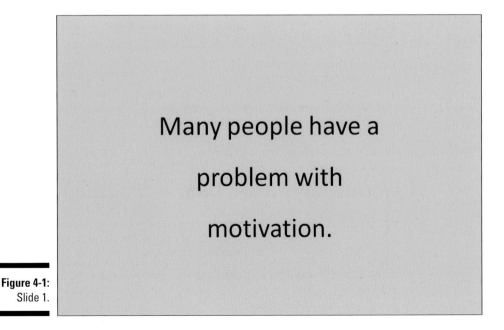

Many people have a

problem with

motivation.

Figure 4-1:
Slide 1.

Figure 4-2:
Slide 2.

Please take a look at them and consider the following questions:

- ✔ How do they affect you?
- ✔ Which one is more effective for you?
- ✔ Which one will remain longer in your memory?

I bet that you prefer slide no. 2 and I'm certain that you'll retain this slide image longer in your memory.

The next time that you listen to a talk accompanied by presentation slides, see which items you notice first when you look at the sheets. If there are visual elements on the slides, I bet that you notice and perceive these first.

A picture says more than a thousand words

Pictures have the following properties:

- ✔ They can be quickly recognised and processed.
- ✔ They are unique. This helps us to memorise them easily and retain them for longer.

✔ They appeal to our emotions.

✔ They provide a lot of information that would be difficult to express by purely linguistic means.

Our brains respond very strongly to pictures. Visual information takes priority over all other information. Neuroscience has a special term for this: the *pictorial superiority effect*. John Medina explains this phenomenon in his book *Brain Rules* by the evolutionary significance of pictures. Once upon a time people retained important (survival) information above all in the form of moving images. Whoever could process these quickly had an advantage. This explains why we react so strongly to pictures today and why visual information is so important for us.

How we think

Without examining neuroscience in any detail, I'd like to explain briefly how people actually think. This provides you with a better understanding of why Mind Mapping works so well. I highlight three points in this regard. Our thinking is:

✔ Unpredictable

✔ Led by association

✔ Orientated towards key concepts

Not sequentially but in leaps and bounds

Do you remember the last meeting you attended? Was there an agenda with points arranged 'one, two and three'? If so, was this agenda adhered to?

If the agenda is adhered to and all points are addressed, then this hardly ever happens in precisely the intended order. Sometimes all it takes is for a keyword to crop up or a colleague to say 'regarding project XY, it seems to me that...', then the agenda is abandoned and you jump to a different place. That's actually quite normal, since people don't think in terms of 'one, two, three', but allow their thought processes to move freely between a number of concepts. This frequently erratic generation of thoughts is due in large part to the way in which people connect information.

Associations – lemon fragrance and . . . ?

In psychology, association is the linking of concepts which evoke each other sequentially. The brain of each person contains millions of associations which have arisen from previous learning experience. If I ask 'what do you associate with the word happiness?', I get 10,000 different answers from 10,000 different people. The past experience of the individual concerned is responsible for what triggers the completely unrelated associations in each person. This explains why it's so easy to drift away from the subject in a discussion.

A little core information instead of a lot of details

Unfortunately, our brains aren't very good at recording a lot of detailed information, especially if it holds little meaning for us. However, we're good at extracting key concepts and basic rules. Often all that's needed are a couple of important key ideas or information to return to the topic or to understand a topic at all. It's often the case that we filter pieces of information important to us out of large amounts of detail. In this sense less is often more.

Mind Mapping as a Brain-Friendly Technique

All the aspects of brain function alluded to so far are combined in the Mind-Mapping technique.

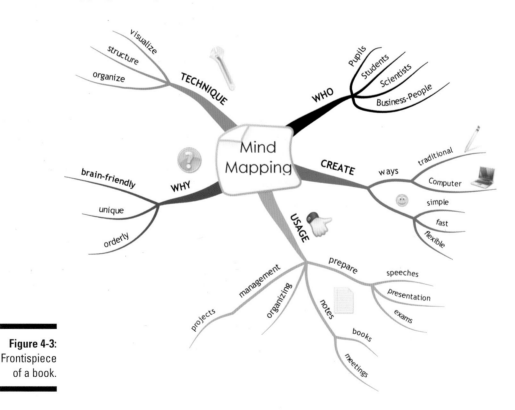

Figure 4-3:
Frontispiece
of a book.

Figure 4-3 contains an example of a Mind Map. You can see that a Mind Map combines the following elements:

- ✔ It's divided into elements that are logical to the author.

- ✔ It presents information hierarchically, just as you would find it in a numbered list. The main branches represent the main points just like the chapter headings of a book.

  Detailed information is found on sub-branches emerging from the main branches. Figure 4-4 illustrates this connection.

- ✔ Important information is written in the form of words or numbers on the branches.

- ✔ Colours add diversity to the Mind Map and have a specific meaning.

- ✔ The Mind Map contains visual elements and is itself like one large picture that you can quickly and easily memorise and understand.

- ✔ Information is also arranged spatially. Important information involving the main theme is placed right by the central idea. Details are given on sub-branches.

  A connected topic is located on the same main branch. This also helps with memorisation.

- ✔ All information is expressed by basic key concepts.

- ✔ The use of branches and key concepts supports the flow of associations.

- ✔ The use of just one keyword per branch means that the Mind Map can be extended flexibly at any time. This is particularly suited to unpredictable thinking. It doesn't matter at which point you want to extend the Mind Map, as it can be done anywhere.

- ✔ The Mind Map is created on plain paper, sideways.

- ✔ The branches and sub-branches are written on wavy, curvy lines, keeping the line length the same as the word length.

You can see that a Mind Map is highly suited to the thought processes in our brains, because information is presented and linked together in a way that makes it easy for the brain to assimilate.

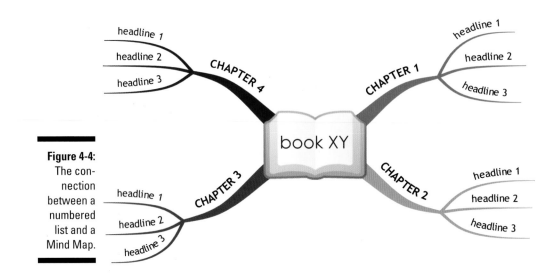

Figure 4-4:
The con-
nection
between a
numbered
list and a
Mind Map.

More Than Just the Sum of its Parts

All these aspects of a Mind Map make it more than the sum of its parts.

The big picture and details

A Mind Map provides an overview of a topic and all the detailed information at the same time. This makes connections and links within a thematic area much clearer. Reading a Mind Map is comparable to using a Google Map. As a viewer you can zoom in on the topic at any time or observe the whole thing from a greater distance.

More information dimensions and greater information density

Unlike pure text, a Mind Map presents several kinds of information simultaneously, making the meaning of a theme a great deal clearer.

Each piece of information in a Mind Map is conditioned by the following aspects:

- ✔ The word on the branch.
- ✔ The position of the branch within the Mind Map.
- ✔ Colours which may carry a particular meaning.
- ✔ Graphic elements which can contain additional meaning.

By having all these layers of information effectively superimposed on each other, the information density of a Mind Map is significantly greater than in a text like this book. This is the only way we can explain how the content of a whole book can be packed into one or several Mind Maps. The superimposed information layers of a Mind Map allow the author of the map to present the theme in an easily comprehensible, sensible and yet highly compact way. However, it usually only works for the person who has drawn up the Mind Map.

What Mind Mapping can't do

Hitherto I have emphasised why Mind Mapping works and what it's good for. Despite its versatility, Mind Mapping is not a panacea. There are situations where it's better to present information in another way.

✔ **Linear information:** Whenever the exact sequence of information is important, a Mind Map is not the ideal means of presentation. An example of this is giving directions. First turn left, then go straight on, then turn right, and only in that order. In Mind Mapping, information isn't arranged linearly but in parallel. A Mind Map is unsuitable for exclusively linear information.

✔ **Process presentations:** In a process chart the sequential arrangement of information is very important. The logic of a process chart isn't the same as a Mind Map's.

✔ **Mathematicalcal expressions:** Formulae and other calculations can't be properly presented in Mind-Map format. Nevertheless, a Mind Map can be used to clarify the connections between thematic areas of mathematics, for example.

Part II

Traditional Mind Mapping in Practice

The 5th Wave — By Rich Tennant

"...and how long have you been practising these speed reading techniques?"

In this part . . .

1 focus on the traditional ways of drawing Mind Maps with pen and paper. In many instances you don't prepare Mind Maps on a computer but draw them by hand in tried and tested fashion. This can even be an advantage. In this part you learn about and practise some classical ways of using Mind Maps.

You discover how you can use Mind Maps to prepare and structure lectures, talks and presentations. Then I explain how Mind Maps can help you take notes from textbooks. Next you switch from written to verbal information, and finally you practise taking notes in talks and meetings.

Chapter 5

Preparing Talks and Lectures Using Mind Maps

. . . .

In This Chapter

▶ Applying Mind Maps to talks and lectures

▶ Learning how to prepare a Mind Map lecture manuscript step by step

▶ Example of a Mind Map lecture manuscript

. . . .

*I*f you've attended a number of talks, lectures and presentations, you may not remember much about any of them. However, you'll no doubt recall that some of them were very good and others rather bad. What's the essence of a good talk or lecture?

One obvious aspect is whether the lecture is delivered in a lively, dynamic way. A lecture that's merely read out doesn't come across very well and as a listener this often seems like a waste of time, especially if it's obvious that it's just being read to you.

Freedom and Flexibility with Mind Maps at All Times

With Mind Mapping you can prepare lecture notes that:

✔ Allow you to speak freely and naturally.

✔ Provide an assurance that you always have all the information you need at your fingertips and haven't forgotten anything.

✔ Contain the points of a lecture or talk on a single page or just a few pages, meaning that you don't need to have a whole sheaf of papers.

Reading mind maps in sequence . . . or not

As I've already shown in Chapter 3, on Mind Mapping rules, there's no fixed sequence in which the main branches of a Mind Map should be read. You can also determine the sequence of all the branches by numbering them, as this figure makes clear.

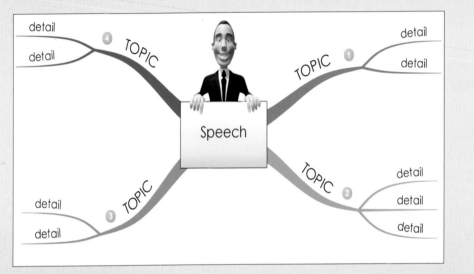

But there's also a natural sequence in which Mind Maps can be read. You start at one o'clock and then work round the Mind Map clockwise. As for the sub-branches of a Mind Map, you start again at the top and also work round them in clockwise fashion. The figure belowt shows how this is done.

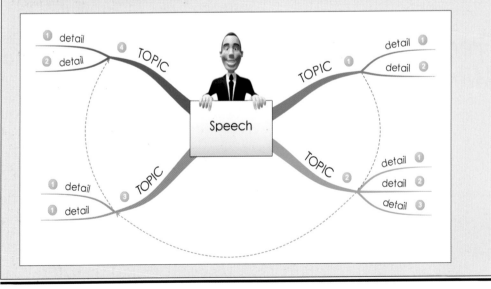

If possible you can do this by using the special ways of drawing Mind Maps presented in Chapter 3.

The great thing about Mind Mapping lecture manuscripts is that:

✔ You can manage content in a particular sequence or abandon this sequence at any time.

✔ You can present some elements elaborately and in detail but pass over others quickly. For example, you can gauge how much detail to provide according to the reactions and knowledge of your audience or how much time you have left.

Use a Mind Map first and foremost as your personal 'crib'. If you're presenting a lecture not only verbally but also graphically, then the Mind Map is no substitute for visualisations used in the lecture and these should be prepared separately.

With Mind-Mapping software, Mind Maps can be displayed in such a way that you can use your manuscript entirely as a prompt for the lecture.

Preparing Lectures: Step by Step

It's usually pretty clear how Mind Maps can be used when you're preparing talk and lecture notes. Check this by presenting one of your Mind Maps to someone else and see how well they understand the content.

I now suggest a procedure for preparing lecture notes step by step with Mind Maps. Imagine that you have to give a 20-minute talk on the topic 'creativity'.

Step 1: Marshalling your initial thoughts

The first step involves assembling your initial ideas and thoughts on the topic and collecting them in Mind-Map format.

First gather together your knowledge of the topic and your ideas about it and visualise them with Mind Mapping. But don't worry about whether you have worked out the *right* or *best* structure for your talk. Step 1 is essentially the basis on which you'll construct your talk.

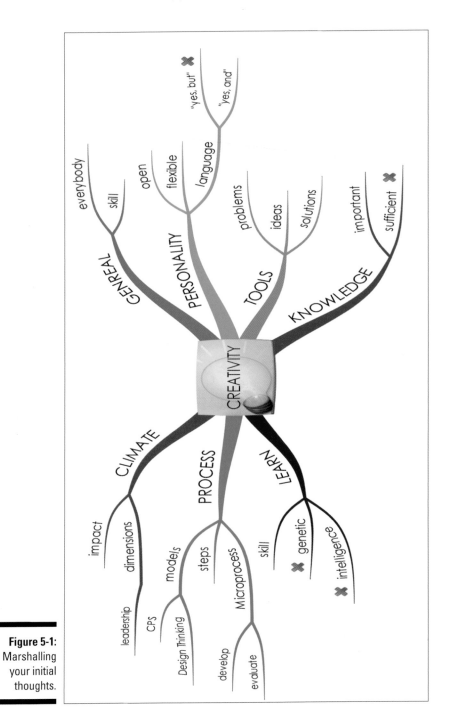

Figure 5-1:
Marshalling
your initial
thoughts.

Figure 5-1 contains a summary of thoughts about creativity prepared with iMindMap software.

Step 2: Determining the main themes

In step 1 you created a foundation of knowledge and ideas that you can rework and refine in the next step to produce a functional manuscript for a lecture or talk.

To turn the content of step 1 into a structure suitable for delivering a lecture you now have to take other structural criteria into account, such as the dramatic aspects of the lecture and the nature of your target audience. You can do this by adapting the content of the Mind Map from step 1.

In light of the above, now think about the potential main branches of the new Mind-Map manuscript which present the main themes of your talk or lecture.

Figure 5-2 shows how this might look for my lecture on creativity.

Another possibility is to divide the Mind Map into rough structural units like introduction, main part and conclusion. This is shown in Figure 5-3.

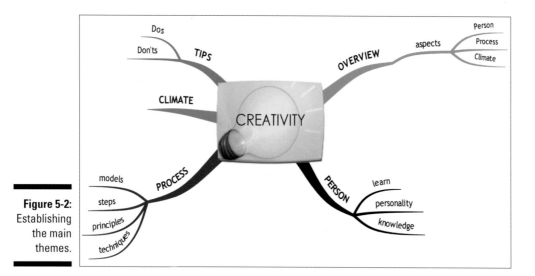

Figure 5-2:
Establishing the main themes.

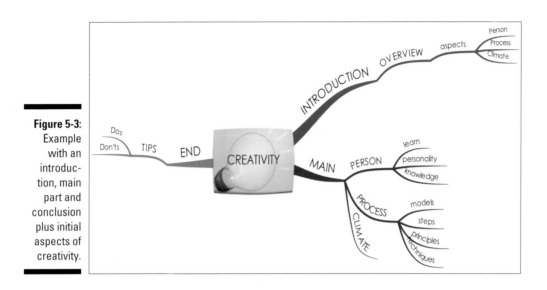

Figure 5-3:
Example
with an
introduc-
tion, main
part and
conclusion
plus initial
aspects of
creativity.

Step 3: Adding detail

Now that you've established the broad outline of your talk you can add as
many details to the main branches as you like.

Details may include the following elements:

✔ Detailed content in the form of sub-branches

✔ Graphic information like symbols and colour coding

Just how detailed your Mind Map turns out to be depends on how familiar
you are with your topic. If you're working in an area that you know very well,
then just a few keywords suffice to make the content presentable. If you're
not so sure about your subject matter, it's sensible to add more details to
your Mind Map to ensure that the information is readily available.

Especially when using Mind Maps as a prop for a talk or lecture, you should
work with many graphic elements and colours, as they're assimilated particularly quickly and easily and more rapidly than words. This means that you
need only glance at your notes briefly and can then devote yourself whole-
heartedly to your audience.

This step involves striking a balance between essential details on the one
hand and not overloading the Mind Map on the other. If you notice that a
Mind Map is becoming too crowded then start another page on which further
content can be added.

Step 4: Testing the Mind Map

Basically it doesn't really matter how you prepare the content of a lecture: but before you deliver the lecture to your audience you should try it out on yourself at least once. This also applies to your Mind Mapping document. By testing it in this way you can:

- ✔ Check whether the Mind Map has enough detail.
- ✔ Determine whether the structure of the Mind Map meets the requirements of the lecture.
- ✔ Practise your lecture so that you feel even more confident when you actually deliver it.

If during the test procedure you notice that some of the branches of the Mind Map are not detailed enough for you, then you still have time to correct this. It may often be the case that you:

- ✔ Find a handier keyword for a branch.
- ✔ Add further details in the form of sub-branches.
- ✔ Incorporate images, symbols and colour codes to add more information and meaning to the Mind Map.

After this test you can of course make further changes to the structure so the Mind Map is ideally suited to your presentation.

And Now for an Example

All theory is dull, so here's an example of a lecture manuscript which I've already prepared.

Figure 5-4 shows a lecture manuscript for a talk lasting around 15 minutes on Taiwan. I gave this lecture some years ago. The Mind Map contains only basic keywords, sufficient for recalling content. As I'd lived there for a year and was intensely involved at that time with the country's politics I didn't need any additional information. The Mind Map is mainly drawn in black and white. The red, green and blue colours stand for various political figures whom I've marked accordingly.

The Mind Map was my personal manuscript, seen only by me and not by my audience. The lecture was accompanied by photos of Taiwan which supported the main theme.

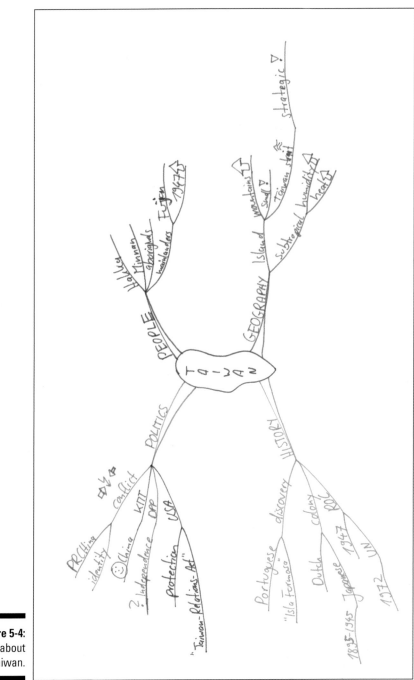

Figure 5-4:
Talk about
Taiwan.

Chapter 6

Handling Text with Mind Mapping

. . . .

In This Chapter

▶ Putting sentences into Mind-Map form

▶ Developing definitions and entering them in Mind Maps

▶ Making Mind-Map notes on a text

▶ Presenting whole books in a Mind Map

. . . .

oesn't it sometimes annoy you that when you read a textbook you almost immediately forget most of its content as soon as you put the book back on the shelf? Wouldn't it be nice to have the content of the entire book at your fingertips on just one or a few pages and be able to dip into it again whenever you want?

Mind Mapping allows you to do precisely that. With Mind Maps you can present textbook content for yourself as author of the Mind Map in a clear and compact way. I stress again that this is predominantly for the benefit of the Mind Map's author. Moreover, the approach presented in this chapter concerns mainly textbooks and specialist texts, because the expectations of most people who approach this kind of writing aren't the same as for prose, which we read merely for enjoyment. In a novel you don't normally have to answer questions or memorise particular content. The opposite applies to textbooks which have to be read for your job or studies.

In this chapter I explain step by step how to get from text to Mind Map.

Converting Text and Sentences into a Mind Map

Be it a two-page newspaper article or a 200-page book, a text consists first and foremost of individual sentences. If they're important to you they have to be converted into a Mind Map. If you master this principle you can then process whole texts as well. In this section I show you first how to extract the most important information from a sentence and then put it into a Mind Map.

Example: Motivation

Assume that you read a text on the subject of motivation and would like to write out the most important content in the form of a Mind Map. I now present a few sentences which I've taken from this text as an exercise.

You've already read a bit of the text on motivation:

- ✔ The first section contained a *definition* of motivation.
- ✔ The second section is now concerned with the *preconditions* for motivation.

I've presented these two themes in Figure 6-1.

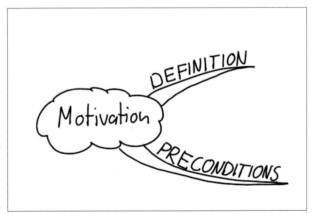

Figure 6-1:
Mind Map –
motivation.

So you've reached the section on the preconditions for motivation which I've already indicated with a main branch in Figure 6-2.

You then encounter the following sentence:

'A precondition for developing motivation is personal interest.'

Now imagine that you have to select just one keyword from this sentence and write it as a sub-branch after your 'preconditions' branch.

I expect you're wondering how to choose the best keyword. Use a process of elimination and first cross out any words that, in your view, add little to the meaning of the sentence.

You'll probably strike out the following words:

- ✔ 'Precondition', since this word is already on the main branch.
- ✔ 'Motivation', since that's the Mind Map's main theme.
- ✔ 'A', 'for' and 'is', as these are words necessary for fluent reading of the text but don't contain any particular meaning.

This leaves you with 'developing', 'personal' and 'interest'.

Which word do you choose to write as a keyword on your sub-branch? There's no obvious rule for this. Which word you choose depends on:

- ✔ How the text is structured.
- ✔ How you interpret the text.
- ✔ What you personally consider to be important.
- ✔ How you've structured the Mind Map so far.

Now take a look at how your Mind Map might appear in each of the three variants.

Variant no. 1: 'Interest'

Figure 6-2 shows how the Mind Map might look if you select the word 'interest'.

Now write the word 'interest' beside the 'preconditions' branch. You can then insert the word 'personal' as a sub-branch of 'interest' and proceed to add further details.

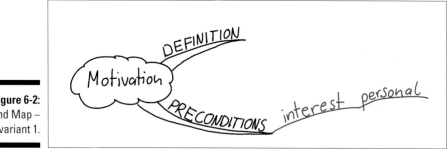

Figure 6-2:
Mind Map –
variant 1.

Variant no. 2: 'Developing'

Figure 6-3 shows how the Mind Map might look if you choose the word 'developing'. I've added further details after the word 'developing'.

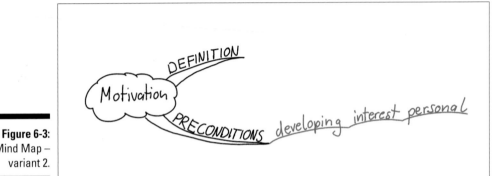

Figure 6-3:
Mind Map –
variant 2.

You've now entered the first sentence in your Mind Map. Next I present another sentence which is also taken from the section *preconditions*:

> *'A further factor in developing motivation is the personal esteem shown by one person to another.'*

Apply the process of elimination here too and cross out any words that you feel don't add significantly to the meaning.

In my opinion the central concepts in this sentence are 'esteem', 'personal' and 'another'.

Again you have to choose from several keywords. In Figure 6-4 I present a possible variant based on Figure 6-3:

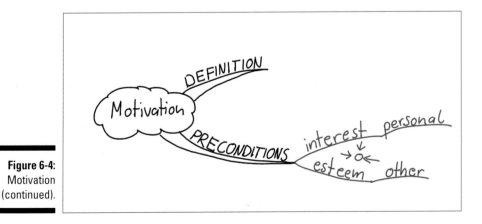

Figure 6-4:
Motivation
(continued).

I've now added 'esteem' as another sub-branch of the 'preconditions' branch. I've also entered a small symbol which tells me that I'm the one being esteemed. On another sub-branch labelled 'esteem' I've put the word 'other' to make it clear that the esteem is directed at me by other people.

Example: Email guideline

Imagine that your company has adopted a new guideline on how emails should be handled in future. It's 40 pages long and you've been chosen to work through it and present it to your colleagues.

The guideline can be divided into two main parts: 'sending emails' and 'receiving emails'. I've entered these in the Mind Map as per Figure 6-5.

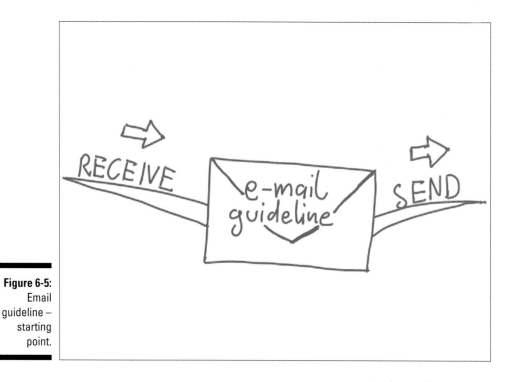

Figure 6-5:
Email
guideline –
starting
point.

You're now in the section 'send'. There you read the following sentence:

'Check whether file attachments are virus-free before sending an email.'

In your view, which words contain the important information?

Students in my classes usually go for 'check', 'file attachments' and 'virus-free'.

In Figure 6-6 I've indicated two alternatives.

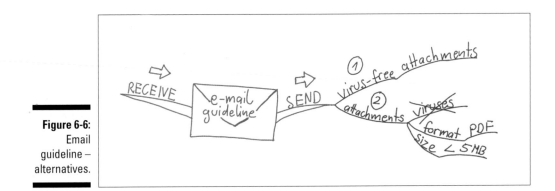

Figure 6-6:
Email
guideline –
alternatives.

Variant no. 1: Virus-free

In this variant the word 'virus-free' is the selected keyword. The exclamation mark after the word means that it's important and I must pay attention to it. It also encompasses the meaning of the word 'check'.

The word 'attachments' is now added as a sub-branch. The email guideline may contain other things that also have to be virus-free. These can also be inserted in the form of sub-branches.

Variant no. 2: Attachments

In the second variant I've chosen the word 'attachments'. This is followed by details in the form of sub-branches. One detail is that attachments must be virus-free. I've expressed this by putting a line through 'viruses'.

In Mind Maps you can indicate a negative by drawing a line through a branch. This means you don't need to write in words like 'no' or 'not'.

In addition to the virus-free aspect, the imaginary email guidelines can also include other items. For example, in future, attachments should only be sent in a particular format, that is, as pdf-files. Moreover, there's an upper limit of five megabytes and this must not be exceeded. All of these elements are reflected in my Mind Map in the form of sub-branches.

By following this approach you can now turn whole texts and books into Mind Maps. Whenever you read information which is important to you, this can be inserted into the Mind Map in the way described above. With a bit of practice it becomes quite automatic and very fast.

Interlude: Scientific Definitions as a Mind Map

Before moving on to deal with a whole text in the next section, I'd like to pause for a moment. I've held many classes for scientists. Initially I always meet the objection that it's all very well processing simple sentences in this way but that it wouldn't work for complex scientific definitions. So I've developed a *definition exercise* to demonstrate that with Mind Maps you can also process texts in which 'every word' is important. This exercise is also good practice for working on whole texts.

Take the following definition of the term *work*, which has to be presented as a Mind Map:

> 'Work: an activity or action that's done in certain contexts and leads to a tangible and/or intangible result which can be evaluated against certain standards; it's effected by applying the physical, mental and intellectual effort of human beings and serves to satisfy their needs.'

Imagine you're preparing a definitions Mind Map for an exam and you need to include different kinds of definitions involving a theme. Figure 6-7 shows the basic structure.

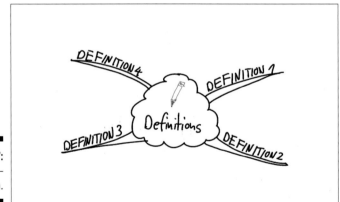

Figure 6-7:
Mind Map –
definition.

Before looking at Figure 6-8, which displays one way of presenting this definition, please try to tackle this definition yourself. You can proceed in the way indicated in Figure 6-7. You place the term 'definitions' in the centre. The word 'work' is added as a main branch to this central idea. The definition then follows.

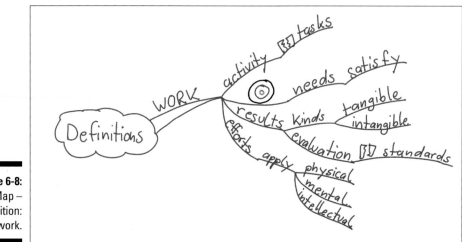

Figure 6-8:
Mind Map –
definition:
work.

Figure 6-8 contains my presentation of the definition as a Mind Map. There are of course other possible ways of structuring the Mind Map.

Perhaps what struck you about this example was that:

✔ I work with a symbol to convey the notion of 'dependent on', for example, an activity that depends on particular tasks.

✔ I use so-called *bridging branches* to improve the structure of a theme. Hence I attach a sub-branch 'kinds' after the branch 'results' to give the Mind Map an even better structure. The word 'kinds' was not in the definition but it helps me to keep a clear view of the map.

✔ I work with a target symbol that in my Mind Maps usually stands alone without keywords and indicates the target or aim of something.

Processing Whole Books with Mind Mapping

Now that you've done some preliminary exercises you're ready to process a whole text and present it as a Mind Map. The text in the nearby sidebar is taken from my classes and is printed out on exactly one side of A4 paper.

If you'd like to learn how to present specialist texts and whole books clearly as one or more Mind Maps, I recommend you do the following exercise.

The myriad benefits of Mind-Mapping

Mind Mapping – the 'Swiss army knife' of working techniques.

Being able to process growing quantities of information continually on subjects of increasing complexity in less and less time characterises the everyday activity of many knowledge workers. And, in an age when knowledge is being rapidly superseded, workers need to be constantly retraining and acquiring new skills.

To be able to cope with all this quicker, better and more effectively, you need various strategies in the form of usable and applicable working techniques to support you. One method which has proven very useful for many people is Mind Mapping as conceived by Tony Buzan. Mind Mapping is a simple but very effective way of visualising, organising and structuring thoughts, knowledge and information. And the best thing about this technique: unlike many other procedures, the way in which Mind Maps operate and are displayed assist the natural thought processes of the brain. Information is presented in different ways (words, colours, pictures, symbols and spatial organisation) at the same time, thereby simplifying mental processing and supporting memorisation and learning.

The few minor but crucial rules for working effectively with Mind Maps are:

✔ Mind Maps always start from a central idea in the middle of the paper.

✔ Like a tree trunk this central idea is surrounded by branches and sub-branches.

✔ As many sub-branches as you like can be attached to the main branches at different levels.

✔ It's important that the branches are always connected to each other and not left floating about unattached.

✔ Sub-branches are always depicted underneath or at the end of a main branch.

✔ Keywords are placed on the branches – just one (!) word is written per branch. This means that a theme can be extended in all directions from just one keyword.

✔ Mind Maps function with symbols, pictures and colours that can also contain further information.

The advantages of this compared with the linear approach are:

✔ The central idea is emphasised more clearly.

✔ The relative significance of content is more obvious at a glance. Important points are placed near the centre with details on sub-branches.

✔ Connections between key concepts are made easily recognisable by connecting lines.

✔ This type of structure enables you to integrate new information easily at any time without disfiguring the map's clarity with deletions and inserted words.

✔ Every Mind Map is unique and individual. That's a great help for the memory.

✔ Visual presentation of a theme makes connections and links more obvious to the viewer.

✔ Mind Maps are quickly generated and recalled.

Since Mind Mapping can be used for anything where information and thoughts need to be structured, organised and displayed, the range of possible applications is very broad. This explains why Mind Maps have also been called the 'Swiss army knife' of working techniques. Now a few examples of how they are deployed:

(continued)

(continued)

- Preparing lectures, articles, presentations and discussions.

- Taking notes in lectures and classes and preparing extracts from books and texts.

- Making records and taking minutes in meetings and talks.

- Visualising problems or marshalling ideas for solutions; discussing such proposals.

- Helping with structuring and organisation in project management.

In recent years a whole range of software applications has been developed to extend the possibilities of traditional Mind Mapping using a pen and paper. With the assistance of software Mind Maps can be altered, manipulated and extended more easily and linked to other digital content. However, computer programs which make Mind Maps or Mind Map-like visualisations possible should not be compared with the Mind Mapping technique itself and software should not be regarded as the successor to pen and paper, thereby superseding the traditional approach. Both pen and paper and software have their own applications and one or the other is used according to the situation concerned. For example, if learning and memorisation are the aim, writing and drawing Mind Maps by hand is more appropriate from a psychological perspective and preferable to a computer. In creative endeavours too, many people find that experimenting and working with a sheet of paper and different pens is the most effective method. On the other hand, software is better suited to project management and importing digital information. Computer-generated Mind Maps can be regarded as a sort of control centre from which all important information can be called up and viewed.

It's rather like driving a car. What car you drive depends on what you need it for and your personal preferences. The important thing is having learned to drive in the first place!

Your task is to present the most important information in this text as a Mind Map. Therefore, the theme of your Mind Map is also 'Mind Mapping'.

The best way of dealing with the text

What's the best way of dealing with the text? Many people suggest the following:

1. Read through the text once in full.

2. Mark the important words.

3. Then generate the Mind Map.

This approach is perhaps still practical for a one-page text. But I guarantee that you won't generate a Mind Map from a whole book by using this procedure. You'd first have to read through the entire book, then mark the important places and finally take notes. Most people wouldn't bother with taking notes after all that, it's just too much effort.

I advise the following approach:

1. **Skim-read the text.** This means that you don't read it in detail but just scan the pages. The aim is to get a basic impression of the structure and organisation of the text and, for example, notice any subheadings and lists of items that can help you to navigate through it.

2. **Read the text in detail and generate a Mind Map at the same time.** Whenever you reach an important point, enter it in your Mind Map. When you've reached the end of the text, your Mind Map will also be complete.

You can always revise your Mind Map later on and that the first version doesn't have to be perfect.

Take about 20 to 25 minutes to prepare and generate the Mind Map.

Good luck with your first note taking with Mind Mapping. Very likely you won't find it so easy on the first occasion and it'll take quite a while. However, it gets quicker and easier each time you try. After a couple of attempts you'll quickly get used to the technique.

Maybe your Mind Map will look something like the one in Figure 6-9, my own notes on the text.

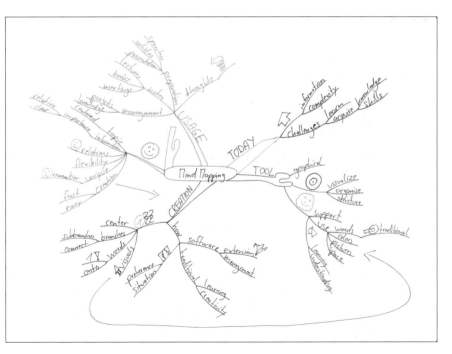

Figure 6-9:
Mind-Map notes on the practice text.

Figure 6-9 displays the content of the text clockwise almost in chronological order:

- ✔ **'Today':** Here I've merged the introduction and preamble.
- ✔ **'Tool':** This contains a definition of the technique and some of its features.
- ✔ **'Creation':** This branch subdivides into the rules – symbolised by the paragraph symbol – and the 'how' branch. I've dealt with the last part of the text here. This was about differentiating traditional Mind Mapping with a pen and paper from Mind Mapping with software.
- ✔ **'Advantages' and 'Usage':** Contain the relevant items from the lists concerned.

As you can see from this example of a Mind Map, the Mind Map doesn't have to reflect the sequence of content in the text. It's up to you where textual content is located within the Mind Map. Structuring your Mind Map may mean that you organise textual content differently from the original arrangement.

If you take notes with a pen and paper, you should ensure that the Mind Map doesn't get too large. Instead, it's better to generate several Mind Maps on the same book and then number them accordingly.

Now you can summarise whole books on just one or a few pages and recall their content to mind in seconds by glancing at the Mind Maps concerned. If you need to work frequently with the content of textbooks, for example because you are a student or need such content for work, this technique is definitely for you.

In addition to a digital or scanned version of my Mind Mapping notes I always keep a copy at the front of the textbook concerned, so that my Mind Map is always to hand.

Chapter 7

Note-Taking in Talks, Lectures and Meetings

Many people frequently encounter situations in which they listen to others and want or need to note something down.

Some examples are:

- ✔ A pupil attends many different classes every day at school.
- ✔ A student goes to lectures as part of his course.
- ✔ An employee takes part in discussions or meetings.

'You only retain what you write down.' The three examples above contain situations in which the individuals concerned probably need or want to write something down. I bet that most people find themselves in situations several times every week where they have to assimilate important information from monologues or dialogues.

Block Text or Mind Map

How do most people extract information from meetings? Although I don't have any scientific statistics on this, I know from personal observation that the majority of people generate traditional *block text*. This means that all information is written down sequentially in a series of lines, forming blocks of text, just like in this book.

Figure 7-1 shows a typical example, such as might arise from a meeting.

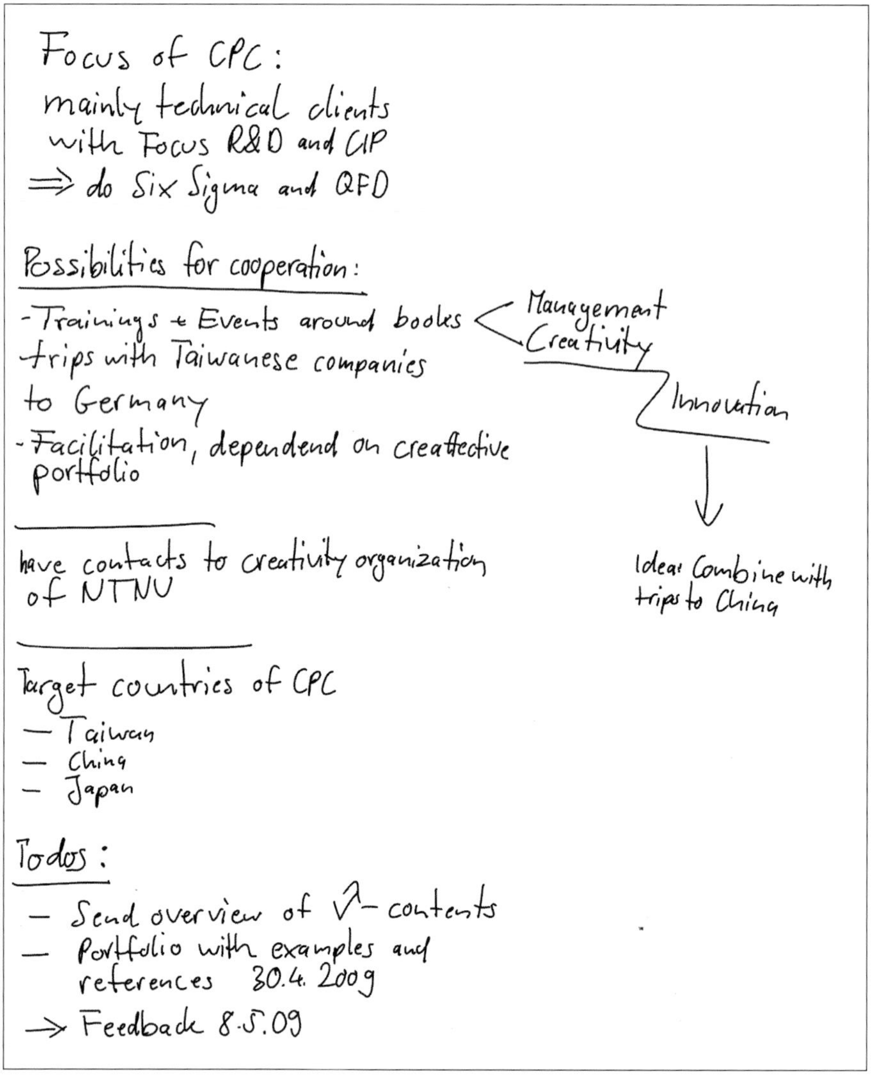

Focus of CPC:
mainly technical clients
with Focus R&D and CIP
⟹ do Six Sigma and QFD

Possibilities for cooperation:
- Trainings + Events around books ⟨ Management
trips with Taiwanese companies   ⟨ Creativity
to Germany
                                   ⟨ Innovation
- Facilitation, dependend on creaffective
portfolio
                                   ↓
have contacts to creativity organization   Idea: Combine with
of NTNU   trips to China

Target countries of CPC
— Taiwan
— China
— Japan

Todos:
— Send overview of ∧-contents
— Portfolio with examples and
references 30.4. 2009
⟹ Feedback 8.5.09

Figure 7-1: Example of traditional note-taking from a meeting.

Now take a look at the same content of meeting notes presented in the form of a Mind Map in Figure 7-2.

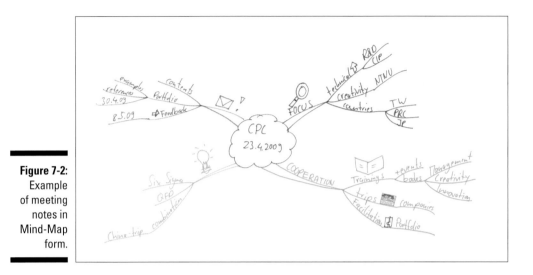

Figure 7-2:
Example
of meeting
notes in
Mind-Map
form.

Figure 7-2 shows notes taken from a 45-minute discussion which I had with a co-operation partner in Taiwan in 2009. It was about collaborating on the presentation of innovation workshops. The individual branches have the following meaning:

- The 'focus' branch indicates the strengths and geographical focus of my partner and target clients.

- The 'cooperation' branch shows which possibilities of collaboration between Germany and Asia we discussed and which were generally feasible for my partner.

- The branch with the light bulb indicates general ideas that occurred to me during the conversation in connection with this partner and the topics discussed.

- The last branch contains two symbols: a letter symbol, which to me means 'send an email', and an exclamation mark, which to me means 'to be actioned'.

Characteristics of talks, lectures and meetings

If you compare Figure 7-1 and Figure 7-2 carefully you notice the following: the sequence of notes in Figure 7-1 doesn't correspond to the order of the Mind Map. This is due to particular aspects of meetings:

✔ People often talk in a disorganised way, jumping from one topic to another. This is due to the association-based way in which our brains operate. A keyword is often enough to call to mind something that's important to us. We then abandon the meeting's clearcut agenda.

✔ Meetings are often disorganised and follow no precise plan.

✔ Unlike text, in a talk or meeting you can't go back to an earlier point or rewind the content.

✔ In contrast to written information, there's no way of knowing the precise structure and composition of the meeting in advance.

The same applies more or less to talks and lectures. Normal note-taking with a pen and paper (but not with a computer) often has the following outcomes:

✔ Information is recorded sequentially in chronological order.

✔ The way in which information is subdivided doesn't correspond to the points in the lecture content, since you can't know its structure beforehand. Elements of content are scattered throughout your notes.

✔ Additions to content at particular points in your notes are usually difficult and have to be squeezed in.

If long and detailed notes need to be taken, your script may appear chaotic and unclear and won't be of much help to you. In my teaching classes many participants admit that block notes of this kind are usually of little value. Many of them say that they often throw away their laboriously taken notes after a while and prefer to learn from books and lecture transcripts, simply because their own notes are unusable.

It's all quite different with Mind Maps. These are characterised by the fact that:

✔ Topics whose content belongs together are located at the right places within a Mind Map.

✔ The chronological order in which information is imparted plays only a minor role in the structure of a Mind Map's content. The way in which Mind Maps are organised means that additions and extensions can be added flexibly to any branch at any time.

✔ The structure – whether imparted by the speaker or imposed by the Mind Map's author – is clear at a glance.

✔ The Mind Map contains just as much or even more information, although less is actually written down. This is because Mind Maps operate only with key concepts, symbols and colours are used and the arrangement of connected branches contains information that would have to be explicitly written out in linear notes.

Of course, the structural content of a Mind Map isn't always perfect, mainly because at the start of a talk or lecture you're unaware of the form it'll take. Nevertheless, you do have structured notes on a theme which you can easily revise later.

Whatever you use your notes for later on, you can always produce a new and improved version. When I use notes only for myself in particular, it doesn't matter whether or not they're perfect.

Give it a try!

In my classes many students are initially sceptical that note-taking can actually be done with Mind Maps. They worry that they won't be able to 'map' fast enough and think that it's still easier to take notes in the old way. Others want to write it all out first and then draw a Mind Map afterwards. However, that's not the point of the exercise: if you generate a Mind Map during the lecture or meeting itself you save yourself duplicated work and also have the information presented in a helpful way.

Therefore, I always set my students an exercise on taking lecture notes so they can see how it works. Afterwards they're really surprised at how well they managed to generate their first lecture Mind Map.

I also invite you to present the content of a documentary in the form of a Mind Map.

Find an interesting documentary on television and, while you're listening, try to draw a Mind Map at the same time. You can start by writing the topic of the documentary in the middle of the paper.

Figure 7-3 shows one way in which a documentary on polar bears can be structured with Mind Mapping.

This is perhaps the first time you've made notes on a documentary, meeting or lecture using Mind Maps. So, how did it go? Was it very hard? Practise a bit more and the technique will become second nature to you.

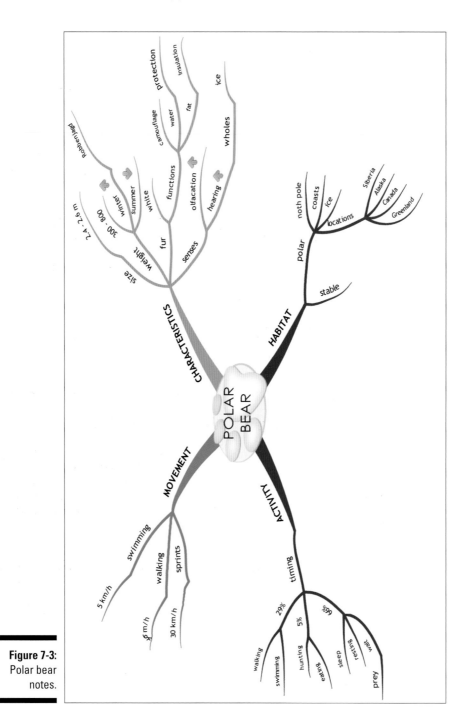

Figure 7-3:
Polar bear
notes.

Colour and symbol codes

It's particularly helpful when making notes on meetings and lectures to have decided on a set of symbols and colours that you can use in your Mind Maps. They have the following advantages:

- ✔ You don't need to write so much and so you save time.

- ✔ You can replace frequently used concepts or themes with symbols, for example, 'priority', 'email', 'phone call', and 'target'. They make it easier for you to recognise and reprocess key information in graphic form when you return to the Mind Map concerned.

- ✔ Combined use of colours and symbols can be especially helpful, allowing you to present several levels of information in a single Mind Map in a very compact way – something that wouldn't be possible in normal note-taking. For example, you can devise colour codes for particular departments or groups whose views you can then connect with them by thematic branches in the appropriate colours.

The colour and symbol codes should make sense and be comprehensible to you and it's not important that they should be obvious to everybody. Choose symbols that work best for you.

Clouds at a local council meeting

In one class I held for council employees, a man had to attend a five-hour council meeting the next day. After the polar bear exercise in class he told me that he intended to try to take notes during this meeting.

Two days later we talked on the phone and he proudly informed me that he made notes on all five hours using Mind Maps and put all the information into just three maps. After the meeting several councillors approached him, curious about the 'clouds' he'd been drawing and wanting to find out what he'd been noting down the whole time and how he did it.

Informative Conversations

Mind Maps are also easily applied to telephone messages. Figure 7-4 contains notes of an initial 20-minute conversation with a prospective customer.

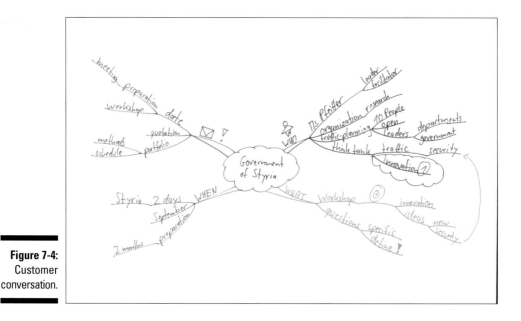

Figure 7-4:
Customer
conversation.

A prospective client called me to see if I could present an innovation workshop for state traffic-safety planners. One technique that I find very helpful for client phone calls is to ask a few well-known journalistic questions such as Who? How? What? When? Where and Why? and use them as main branches. This makes structuring the Mind Map very easy. Whenever a point refers specifically to one of these questions, I can add it to the map. A branch may also have the letter symbol or exclamation mark associated with it. These symbolise things which I have to write in emails and send to clients.

Just Write It Out – Using Your Wandering Thoughts

The American Psychological Association conducted a survey into what people think when they're sitting in a meeting or listening to a lecture. These are the results in figures:

✔ 18 per cent are listening to the speaker.

✔ 25 per cent are having erotic thoughts.

✔ 57 per cent are thinking of something else altogether.

I suppose that these figures should be treated with the same caution as figures on communication and speaking published since the 1970s. According to these, the content of a lecture affects only 7 per cent of listeners, whereas 38 per cent are influenced by the speaker's voice and 55 per cent by their posture.

And yet there's definitely something in these figures.

We know that people don't concentrate on one thing for very long but their thoughts easily wander or that what's said triggers further associations in us which lead to other themes.

Instead of feeling guilty because you can't concentrate for long, you should use your wandering mind as a source of useful associations.

Recording things in block text doesn't make good use of your wandering thoughts or digressions.

This is why the *'just write it out'* technique was developed.

It works like this:

✔ Draw a line down the middle of a sheet of paper, dividing it into two halves. The left side is headed 'in' and the right side 'out'.

✔ Write down everything coming in, that is, what the speaker says, quite normally on the left-hand side under 'in'.

✔ All further thoughts and connections that you consider valuable but don't come from the meeting or talk itself can then be jotted down under 'out' on the right-hand side.

The procedure is a linear format. Linear format means that all information is listed sequentially in exactly the way you hear it. This means that later on you'll have to hand not only information on the lecture but also your own associations drawn from it.

Mind Mapping = in – out to the power of ten

The 'in – out' technique is much more effective if it's applied using Mind Mapping.

In fact, I've mentioned this once already: if you make Mind-Mapping notes in talks or meetings you can mark in your own thoughts and add them to the corresponding branch and content in the map. You can use the following things for 'out-thoughts':

✔ A particular colour reserved only for your own ideas and thoughts. I use orange for this.

✔ A special symbol, for example a light bulb.

Figure 7-5 shows how you can apply the 'in – out' technique using Mind Maps.

By using Mind Mapping in combination with the 'in – out' technique you can combine the advantages of both methods.

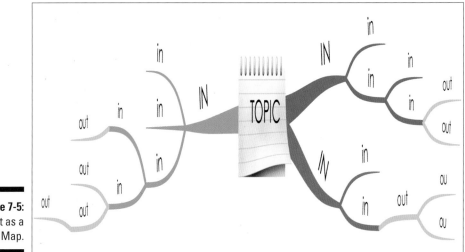

Figure 7-5:
In – out as a
Mind Map.

Part III
Mind Mapping Software

The 5th Wave   By Rich Tennant

"Can't I just give you riches or something?"

In this part . . .

For some time now many people have been acquainted with Mind Mapping in the form of a software package and even think that Mind Mapping is only a computerised technique. But the important thing is to master this technique first, since only then does using software make sense. In this part I shed some light on the increasing number of programs available in this area.

I take a look at many of the available programs, both desktop and web-based varieties, and help you decide between them. In Chapters 11 and 12 I present two programs in detail.

Chapter 8

Software versus Traditional Mind Mapping

○ ○

In This Chapter

▶ Drawing Mind Maps with pen and paper or with a software package

▶ The benefits of Mind-Mapping software

▶ How to decide which method is the best for you

○ ○

*I*f you key 'Mind Mapping' into your Internet browser you'll get more hits for Mind-Mapping software than for the Mind-Mapping technique itself. Hence it's not surprising that many people believe that Mind Mapping is actually the use of a particular Mind-Mapping software package.

Mind Mapping is a technique that enables you to visualise, structure and organise thoughts and information. Like writing itself, Mind Mapping isn't tied to a particular medium (paper or software) and Mind Maps can be generated with either a pen and paper, or with suitable software. The thing that makes both approaches work successfully is knowledge of the technique itself.

Possessing some Mind-Mapping software doesn't necessarily mean that you can work effectively with the technique. You'll most likely use it to generate grid diagrams resembling Mind Maps; however, you'll not yet be in a position to take notes in a meeting or prepare an excerpt from a book. To do this you need an understanding of the technique itself.

Software versus Pen and Paper – The Main Differences

The initial differences are basically of a visual nature. This becomes clear if you take a look at Figures 8-1 to 8-3.

All three Mind Maps deal with the topic of 'Mind Mapping'. Figure 8-1 shows a map drawn by hand. Figure 8-2 shows the same item generated with iMind-Map software, which has a special position in Mind-Mapping programs because it's one of the few Mind-Mapping programs that can arrange the branches of a Mind Map as freely as you would by hand. Figure 8-3 shows a version generated with the Mindjet MindManager software package.

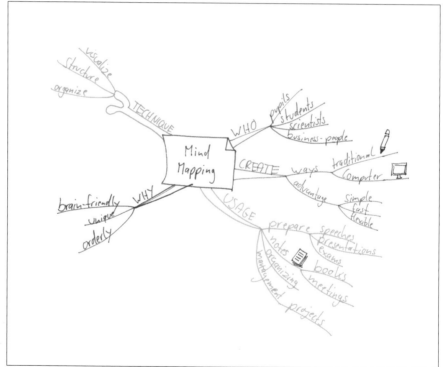

Figure 8-1:
Mind Map
drawn with
a pen and
paper.

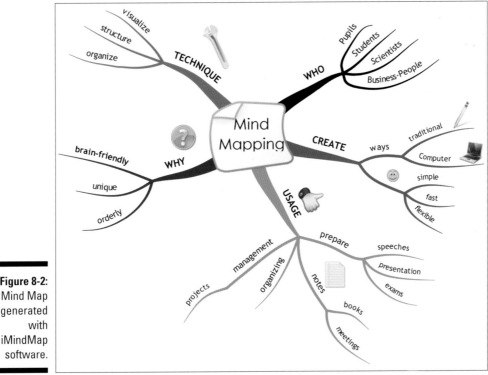

Figure 8-2: Mind Map generated with iMindMap software.

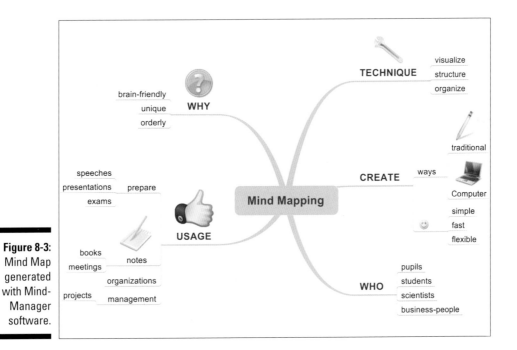

Figure 8-3: Mind Map generated with Mind-Manager software.

Mind Maps generated with Mind-Mapping software and those drawn by hand differ from each other visually in the following ways:

- **Flexible organisation of branches:** With a pen and paper you can, of course, arrange the entire content of the Mind Map in any form you choose, by adding graphics, symbols, and so on.

  Most Mind-Mapping software programs draw in the branches for you and arrange them automatically.

- **Individual versus uniform appearance:** Mind Maps drawn by hand have an individual character. The more graphic elements you use, the more personalised a Mind Map becomes. Software-generated Mind Maps mostly look like the one in Figure 8-3. Of course, you can use software to change colours and to add graphics and symbols, but the results still look similar. This is because you're usually unable to design the branches individually. However, iMindMap software has the additional feature of allowing you to draw in branches 'free hand' (see Figure 8-2).

The advantages of Mind-Mapping software over pen and paper

Although you have little control over the visual appearance of Mind Maps with most computer programs, these do have a number of advantages:

- Mind Maps can be flexibly altered and reworked at any time.
- By using hyperlinks you can access the internet or other files.
- Filtering makes Mind Maps even more flexible.
- Text memos add further information to each branch.
- Mind Maps can be exported to other formats.

In this section I take a closer look at some of these advantages.

Mind Maps can be flexibly altered and reworked at any time

Just as when you compose text on a computer, it's quite straightforward to alter the structure of a Mind Map if you make a mistake or change your mind and to arrange some branches differently. Moreover, graphics and symbols can be changed at any time. Hence it's a good idea to use Mind-Mapping software for tasks that involve frequently changing data, for example, in project management.

Accessing the internet or other files with hyperlinks

Mind-Mapping software allows you to connect a branch with any website or data file via a hyperlink. For example, if you draw a Mind Map for redecorating your house and want to include quotations from painters and decorators, you can easily link the relevant files to your Mind Map. By means of this function Mind-Mapping software allows you to utilise a range of digital information from a Mind Map by linking it quickly to the relevant documents.

This opens up applications of Mind Maps that would scarcely be possible with a pen and paper, for example, project and knowledge management.

If a Mind Map gets too large and unclear, software can divide parts of it into so-called sub-maps. These sub-maps can then be easily linked to the master map via a hyperlink. Figures 8-4 and 8-5 contain an example of this principle. Figure 8-4 shows a map summarising notes taken from a book. All the chapters are mentioned and basic detail of each chapter is given. Each of the main branches links to further detailed maps. Figure 8-5 displays one such detailed map for the chapter 'Patterns' from Figure 8-4.

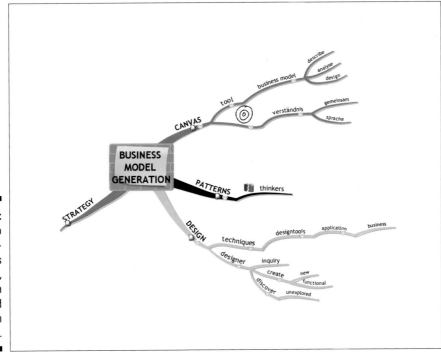

Figure 8-4: Mind Map summarising notes from a book, partly in German and partly in English.

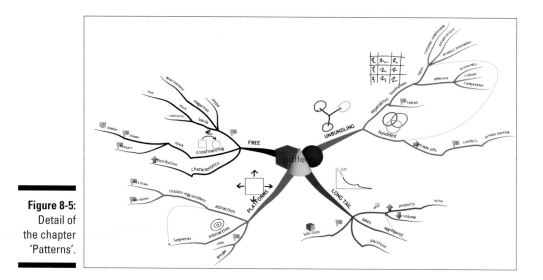

Figure 8-5:
Detail of
the chapter
'Patterns'.

Filtering means even greater flexibility

Some packages like MindManager enable you to filter a Mind Map according
to specific criteria. For example, you can display only those branches which
satisfy a criterion set by you, such as a colour or symbol. In this way you can
generate extracts from a Mind Map and reduce an originally detailed Mind
Map to just a few branches. This function also creates new applications of
Mind Mapping that go far beyond the possibilities of pen and paper.

Text memos add further information to each branch

A feature of Mind Mapping is that only one keyword is ever used per branch.
This leaves a lot of space within the map and branches are slender and clear.

It may sometimes happen that you'd like to write in more material, for
example if you wish to record longish quotations in book notes or you want
to make a Mind Map self-explanatory by writing additional text next to individual keywords.

Mind-Mapping software has a text-memo function for this. You can use it
to enter additional text memos on a branch via an input window. When the
window is closed, the software indicates with a symbol that there are text
memos connected with the branch concerned. You can then open them
at will.

Exporting to other formats

Mind-Mapping software allows you to export your Mind Map to other file
formats for further processing or for people who don't use Mind-Mapping
software.

Most software programs have a number of export functions. Almost all of them can export a Mind Map as a pdf or image file, so anyone can look at it on their computer.

Many packages also allow you to transfer a Mind Map in traditional list format for it to be further processed by other programs. Many programs enable you to generate Word files from a Mind Map. This can be useful, for example, if you prepare Mind-Map notes of a meeting and then want to make a full transcript of them.

Mind-Mapping Software = Mind Mapping Reloaded

You can see that Mind-Mapping software allows you to do more than just display and structure information that's possible in traditional Mind Maps by using a pen and paper. Software and computer functions also enable project and knowledge management which would otherwise be impossible.

Some packages also enable you to collaborate over the internet so several people can work on a Mind Map at the same time, for example. The future of software packages is definitely headed in this direction. Software such as iMindMap (the name has nothing to do with Apple) is also available for iPhones and iPads, meaning that digital Mind Maps can now be produced anywhere.

Whether or not you work with software depends on a number of factors:

  ✔ Your personal preferences.

  ✔ Your readiness to part with money to obtain a software package.

  ✔ The basic conditions in force in your company.

  ✔ The use for which Mind Mapping is intended.

A package that offers many new facilities isn't always the best option. Despite all the progress in computer technology, the act of producing Mind Maps by hand is considered quite special from a psychological perspective. On a computer you usually generate Mind Maps with a mouse and keyboard. However, Mind Mapping with a pen and paper involves the sensory experience of actually writing and drawing (you're using your 'muscle memory' to help you memorise and retain information – see Chapter 13). In this way you assimilate content much more readily than by generating Mind Maps on a computer. Hence there are occasions when I recommend that you still work with a pen and paper.

Drawing Mind Maps by hand is particularly appropriate when learning and memorising are involved, for example:

✔ When preparing for an exam.

✔ When making notes from a book whose content you wish to retain.

Seminar participants tell me again and again that in a meeting it's easier or more acceptable to make notes with a pen and paper than having an open screen in front of you.

On the other hand, there are also some uses to which software is especially suited. This is the case when content frequently changes, for example:

✔ In project management.

✔ If you want to carry on working on a Mind Map in another format.

The important thing to realise is that both ways of producing Mind Maps have their uses and that the main thing is to understand what Mind Mapping is about. Then you can work with software or a pen and paper, as the situation requires.

Chapter 9

Taking a Tour of Mind-Mapping Software

A few years ago the number of software programs for Mind Mapping was still quite manageable, but packages promoted to consumers as Mind-Mapping programs have recently proliferated. It's getting increasingly difficult to keep track of them all and really hard to choose the right one.

In this chapter I shed some light on the issue, present a small selection of programs and provide you with a bit of help with deciding which to buy. If you're interested in using Mind-Mapping software, it would ultimately be a good idea if you tested and tried out some of them for yourself.

Suggested Programs – Genuine Mind Mapping

If something is labelled as a Mind Map, it doesn't necessarily mean that it's one. In this book you've already learned what characterises a real Mind Map. The software programs presented in this chapter are a filtered selection of packages with which you can generate genuine Mind Maps or visualisations that are graphically reminiscent of Mind Maps. Other *visualisation programs* which would like to jump on the Mind-Map marketing bandwagon but don't generate Mind Maps are not included in this list.

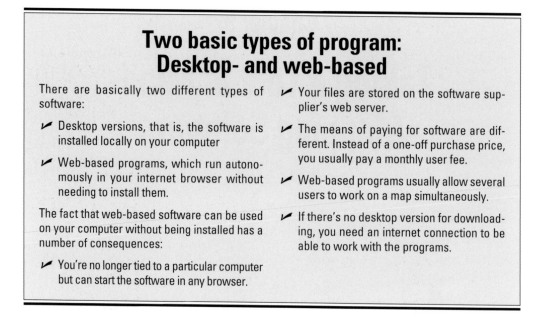

Two basic types of program: Desktop- and web-based

There are basically two different types of software:

🗸 Desktop versions, that is, the software is installed locally on your computer

🗸 Web-based programs, which run autonomously in your internet browser without needing to install them.

The fact that web-based software can be used on your computer without being installed has a number of consequences:

🗸 You're no longer tied to a particular computer but can start the software in any browser.

🗸 Your files are stored on the software supplier's web server.

🗸 The means of paying for software are different. Instead of a one-off purchase price, you usually pay a monthly user fee.

🗸 Web-based programs usually allow several users to work on a map simultaneously.

🗸 If there's no desktop version for downloading, you need an internet connection to be able to work with the programs.

Competition for the attention of target customers means that, just like in other areas, programs are increasingly similar in terms of functionality and appearance and it's getting harder and harder for prospective buyers to see and understand how they differ from each other. The wording of manufacturer websites is sometimes quite interchangeable.

Overview of Desktop Programs

To provide you with an overview of the software programs available and to give you an idea of the kind of Mind Maps that can be generated with the packages concerned, I now present each program with a short description and a diagram.

Aviz Thoughtmapper

Aviz Thoughtmapper (Figure 9-1) is a PC program for generating simple displays which resemble Mind Maps. The examples shown at the website are entirely text-based and don't include graphic elements.

According to the manufacturer there are export functions to MS Office programs and synchronisation with Outlook.

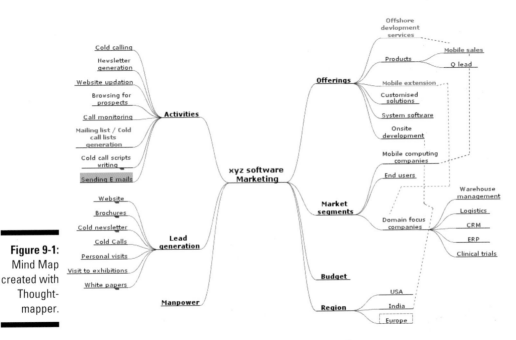

Figure 9-1:
Mind Map
created with
Thought-
mapper.

Website: www.avizsoft.com/thoughtmapper.htm

Concept Draw MindMap

Concept Draw MindMap (Figure 9-2) is a visually appealing Mind-Mapping program for generating Mind-Map-like visualisations on PCs and Macs. The program offers a large number of import and export functions and comes in two versions: Concept Draw MindMap and Concept Draw MindMap for Projects. The latter is a version with functions that are especially useful for project managers.

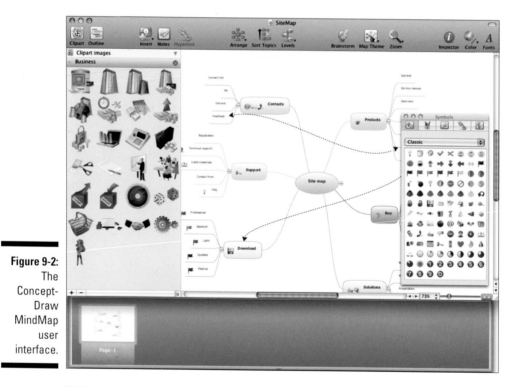

Figure 9-2:
The Concept-Draw MindMap user interface.

Website: www.conceptdraw.com/en/products/mindmap/main.php

EMINEC MYmap

EMINEC MYmap (Figure 9-3) is a simple Mind-Mapping program that has a special brainstorming facility and encryption function.

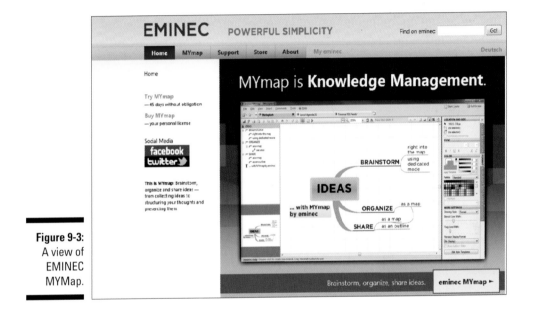

Figure 9-3:
A view of
EMINEC
MYMap.

Website: http://eminec.com

freemind – really free

freemind is one of the most widely-used programs that can run on three platforms: PC, Mac and Linux. The reason for its widespread appeal is the price: freemind is free. Visually, freemind is modelled on Mindjet MindManager (see Figure 9-4).

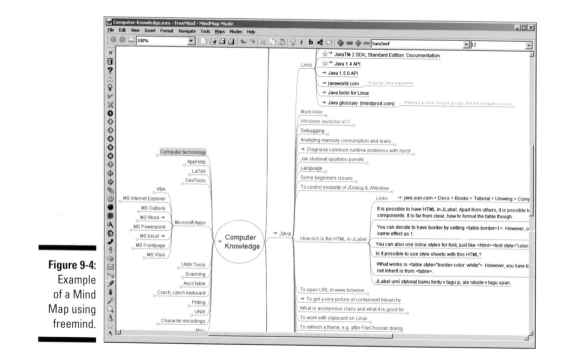

Figure 9-4: Example of a Mind Map using freemind.

Website: http://freemind.sourceforge.net

iMindMap – from the inventor of Mind Mapping

iMindMap (Figure 9-5) is stirring up the Mind-Mapping software market. It was started by Tony Buzan, the inventor of Mind Mapping. iMindMap stands out from the crowd by being one of the few programs that can generate Mind Maps looking like they've been drawn by hand. All other programs generate stark-looking 'fishbone' diagrams. I've devoted a whole chapter to iMindMap in this book, see Chapter 11.

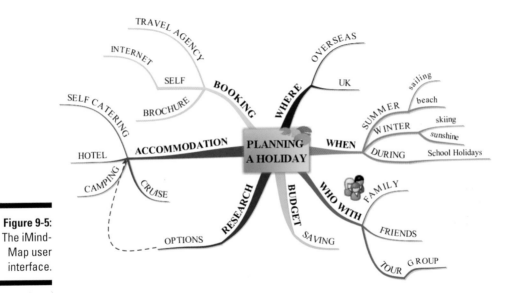

Figure 9-5:
The iMind-
Map user
interface.

Website: www.imindmap.com

Inspiration – recommended for schools

With Inspiration (shown in Figure 9-6) you can create Mind Maps and other map-like visualisations. According to the manufacturer's website, Inspiration has been specially tailored for schools and schoolchildren. There's a child-orientated package called kidspiration for younger pupils.

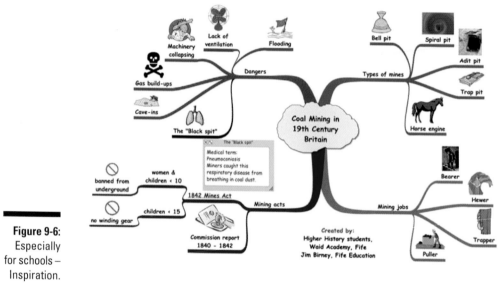

Figure 9-6:
Especially for schools – Inspiration.

World History Analysis Mind Map: Coal Mining in 19th Century Britain

Manufacturer's website: www.inspiration.com

MindGenius

MindGenius (Figure 9-7) claims on its website that this package can create Mind Maps without being hampered by traditional Mind-Map and Mind-Mapping rules. The target audience for this software is the business world.

Figure 9-7:
A collection of ideas with MindGenius.

Manufacturer's homepage: www.mindgenius.com

Mindjet MindManager – the market leader

MindManager was one of the first Mind-Mapping programs on the market and is the market leader worldwide. Its popularity is underscored by the fact that other suppliers of Mind-Mapping software produce import and export functions for MindManager. It's certainly among the more powerful and comprehensive of programs and is characterised by particularly close integration with Microsoft Office products. It's increasingly orientated towards project management based on the Mind-Mapping technique. Together with Mindjet Connect, MindManager provides a service enabling online collaboration among several users. In addition to iMindMap, I also deal with MindManager in a separate chapter, see Chapter 10. Figure 9-8 shows a Mind Map created using MindManager.

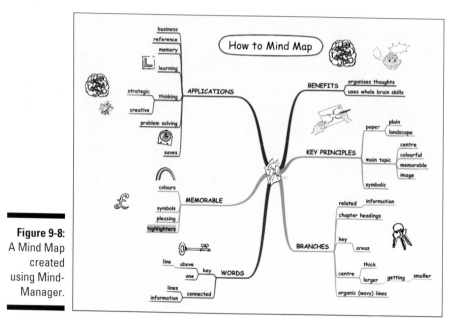

Figure 9-8:
A Mind Map created using Mind-Manager.

Manufacturer's website: www.mindjet.com

MindVisualizer – particularly simple

MindVisualizer (Figure 9-9) is a visually appealing package that is particularly simple and very user-friendly.

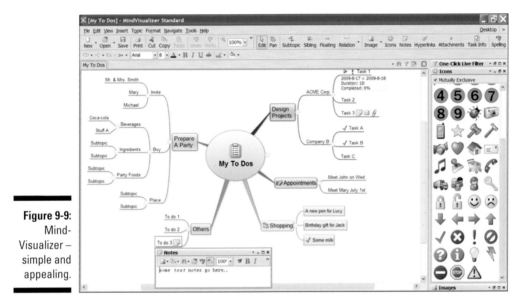

Figure 9-9:
Mind-
Visualizer –
simple and
appealing.

Website: www.innovationgear.com/mind-mapping-software/

MindMapper

MindMapper is a comprehensive and very versatile package that can produce Mind Maps in a variety of layouts (see Figures 9-10 and 9-11) – both with the widespread 'fishbone' design and with an 'artistic look' reminiscent of hand-written Mind Maps. The program is also characterised by a sophisticated brainstorming facility which enables you to marshal your ideas, group them and then integrate them into Mind Maps.

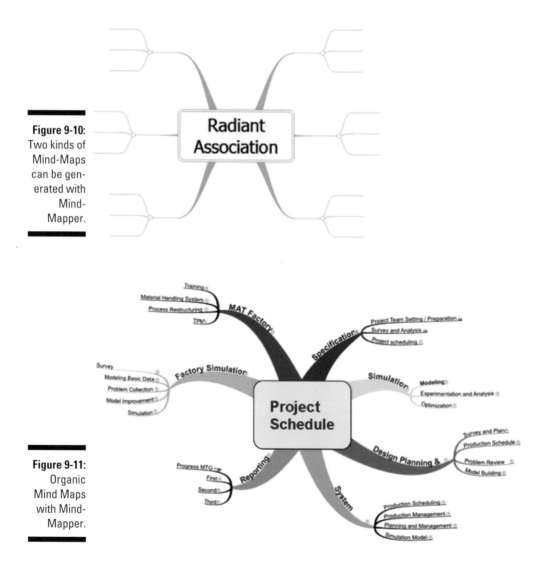

Figure 9-10: Two kinds of Mind-Maps can be generated with Mind-Mapper.

Figure 9-11: Organic Mind Maps with Mind-Mapper.

Website: www.mindmapper.com

Novamind

According to the manufacturer's website you'll be wowed by Novamind. In fact, Novamind is a comprehensive software package with project-management functions and great versatility for generating Mind Maps. See Figure 9-12.

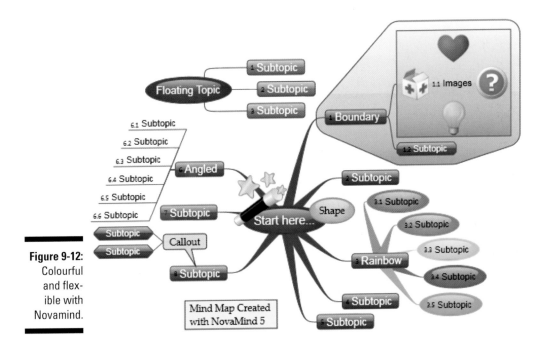

Figure 9-12: Colourful and flexible with Novamind.

Website: www.novamind.com

Matchware MindView 3

MindView (Figure 9-13) also offers a wide range of functions that go beyond mere visualisation and make project-management software really interesting. The user finds it particularly easy to switch between different Mind-Map layouts.

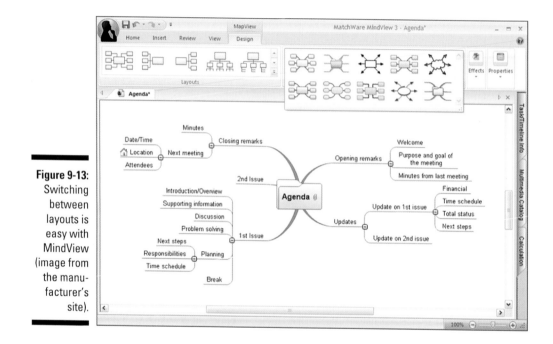

Figure 9-13: Switching between layouts is easy with MindView (image from the manufacturer's site).

Website: www.matchware.com/ge/products/mindview/default.htm

XMind – the basic version is free

XMind (shown in Figure 9-14) is an open-source package. This means that the source code can be viewed and further developed by anyone. The program is available in a reduced-function version free of charge and in a Pro-Version for payment.

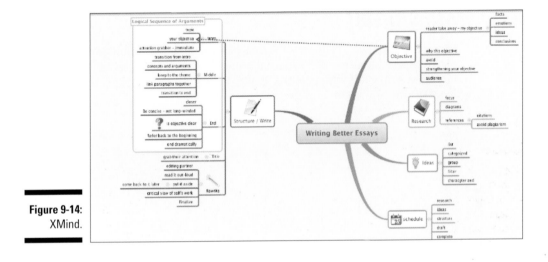

Figure 9-14:
XMind.

Website: www.xmind.net

Web-Based Mind-Mapping Programs

The list of web-based Mind-Mapping programs is more manageable than that for desktop versions, but the trend is definitely towards more and more online programs.

Mapmyself

Mapmyself (shown in Figure 9-15) looks and is used like iMindMap, although the two manufacturers are apparently unconnected. The special thing about Mapmyself, like iMindMap, is the facility to generate Mind Maps that look like hand-drawn examples.

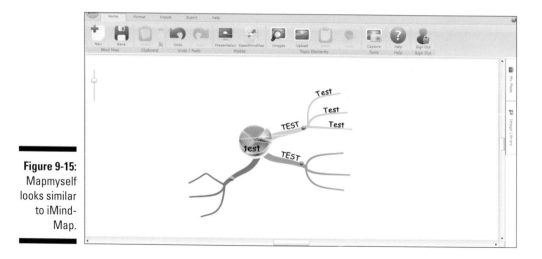

Figure 9-15:
Mapmyself looks similar to iMind-Map.

Website: www.mapul.com

Mind42 – simple and free of charge

Mind42 (see Figure 9-16) is a simple web package for drawing basic Mind Maps. The main thing about this software is the price – it's absolutely free.

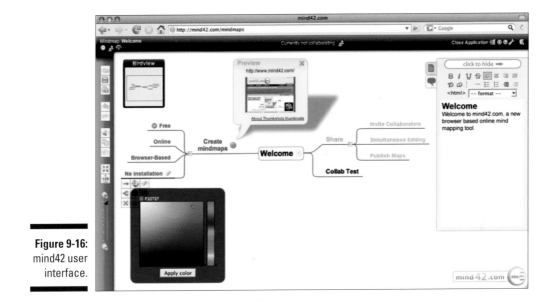

Figure 9-16: mind42 user interface.

Website: www.mind42.com/

MindMeister

MindMeister (Figure 9-17) is one of the first ever online Mind Mapping programs. Very easy to use, it can generate Mind Maps quickly and effectively.

MindMeister is characterised by cute add-ons, for example, an offline facility and browser enhancements for the quick incorporation of sudden ideas.

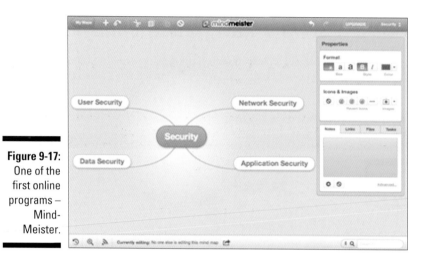

Figure 9-17:
One of the
first online
programs –
Mind-
Meister.

Website: www.mindmeister.com

Mindomo

Mindomo (Figure 9-18) is strongly reminiscent of a slimmed-down web version of Mindjet MindManager, in terms of both user interface and the Mind Maps it generates.

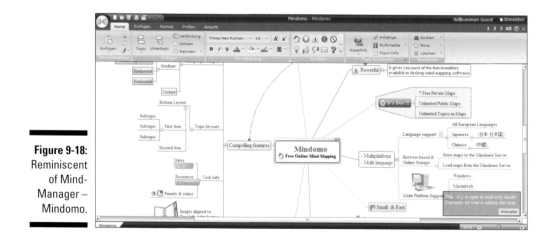

Figure 9-18:
Reminiscent
of Mind-
Manager –
Mindomo.

Website: www.mindomo.com/

Comparing Software Packages

Table 9-1 provides an overview of all the programs mentioned in this chapter. Check the websites for up-to-date prices.

Table 9-1	Summary of Mind-Mapping Programs			
Name	*Versions*	*Operating Sytem*	*Type*	*Organic Mind Map Layout Possible*
Aviz Thoughtmapper		W	Desktop	No
ConceptDraw MINDMAP	MINDMAP MINDMAP for projects	W, M	Desktop	No
EMINEC MYMap	Starter Express Professional Academic	W	Desktop	No
Freemind		W, M, L	Desktop	No
iMindMap	Elements Professional Ultimate Ultimate Plus	W, M	Desktop	Yes
Inspiration		W, M	Desktop	Yes
Mapmyself	Basic Premium		Online	Yes
Mind42			Online	No
Mindomo	Basic Premium Team		Online	No
MindGenius	Education Business	W	Desktop	No

(continued)

Table 9-1 *(continued)*

Name	Versions	Operating Sytem	Type	Organic Mind Map Layout Possible
MindMeister	Basic Premium Business		Online	No
MindManager 9		W, M Sharepoint	Desktop, possibility of online collabora-tion	No
MindVisualizer		W	Desktop	No
MindMapper	Standard Professional Academic USB	W	Desktop	Yes
Novamind	Express Pro Platinum	W, M	Desktop	No
Matchware MindView	Standard Business	W, M	Desktop	No
XMind	Standard Pro	W, M	Desktop	No

(W = Windows, M = MAC OS, L = Linux)

You can see that the choice of packages is large. If you've generated your list of favourite options, download a test version of all packages in which you're interested and then make your choice.

Chapter 10

Introducing Mindjet MindManager

*I*n Chapter 9, I introduced you to the wide range of Mind-Mapping software available. However, in this book I shall limit myself to just two programs, one of them being version 9 of Mindjet's MindManager. In this chapter I am working with the Windows version of the program. Some of the user instructions work only with the Windows version and not with the MAC version.

Why this particular program?

✔ MindManager is the most widely used software package, especially by businesses, and its use is free at many universities in the German-speaking world. So, this program might also be relevant to you.

✔ I've been working with it for many years.

✔ MindManager is the archetype for many other Mind-Mapping programs whose functions and style are based on it.

This chapter focuses on MindManager version 9, which came out in August 2010 and has a more general interface.

MindManager 2012 was released in September 2011 and includes real-time co-editing, enhanced information maps and a new desktop interface, plus new brainstorming features that guide users to unleash their creativity. This version is particularly for business, professional use and incorporates Mindjet's cloud-based service to provide open and full sharing of MindManager maps with anyone, anywhere, on any device. You can find out more at www.mindjet.com/mindmanager.

The Basics: Finding Your Way Around

In terms of its design, MindManager is orientated towards Microsoft Office. If you use Office, then many of its features will be familiar to you. Figure 10-1 shows the start screen.

I'd like to draw your attention to the following functions:

- **Map area:** This takes up most of the screen. This is where you work on your maps.

- **Symbol bars:** These are located in the upper part of the screen and are organised in a way similar to Microsoft Office. The seven categories 'file', 'start', 'insert', 'check', 'view', 'export' and 'extras' provide access to most of the program's functions.

- **Workbook Tabs:** Depending on your settings, these registers are located directly above or below the map area and contain the names of opened maps. If you've several maps open at the same time, several Workbook tabs are also displayed.

- **Task pane:** This tab is normally located to the right of the screen and contains further tabs providing access to resources, icons and images.

- **Status bar:** The status bar is situated beneath the map area and allows you to access important functions like zoom, Gantt diagram and filter.

Figure 10-1: Mind-Manager's start screen.

Important control keys

To be able to work efficiently with Mind-Mapping software it's important that you can add branches quickly and easily to a Mind Map. This is best done with the keyboard. So, you need to memorise the following control keys:

- ✔ **Enter/space key:** Adds a new branch on the same level. For example, if you're at main-branch level, another main branch is inserted.

- ✔ **Insert:** Inserts a new branch at a deeper level. So, if you're at main-branch level and press Insert, a new sub-branch is generated next to the branch you have highlighted.

- ✔ **Remove:** If you press this key, the highlighted branch and all sub-branches are deleted. You can tell if a branch has been highlighted by the blue box appearing round it.

In the task info Task Pane MindManager has a tab marked Learning Centre. Here you'll find video clips helping you to familiarise yourself with the program.

Experiment a little with MindManager and the main control keys to gain confidence and speed.

MindManager automatically organises the branches of a Mind Map for you. So you don't have to worry about having enough room, since you'll never run out of space. However, one consequence of this is that Mind Maps can quickly get out of hand and become unclear. If you have trouble keeping track of it all you should consider dividing your Mind Map into a number of sub-maps.

Keeping it neat and tidy: Formatting options

MindManager gives you everything you need to generate a Mind Map with the same clarity you'd achieve with a pen and paper. This means that you can control the following aspects:

- ✔ **Branch shape, thickness and colour:** The program provides you with a choice of different layouts.

- ✔ **Script colour, size and type.**

- ✔ **Borders:** Colours and other options: here too you can choose from among a number of different layouts. If you place a border around a branch, the highlighted branch and all its sub-branches are enclosed. MindManager's border function also allows you to insert curly brackets after a branch and to add other branches after the brackets.

✔ **Icons:** Via the Library tab in the Task Pane MindManager provides access to a large number of icons. You can attach as many as you like to a branch. You can filter icons but not images.

✔ **Images:** Also via Library MindManager provides a number of pre-categorised pictures; you can attach one of these to each branch. Unlike icons, images can be adjusted for size but not filtered. In addition to pre-categorised images you can also embed graphics files, such as company logos, in a Mind Map.

You can modify all these options via the start symbols bar in the Script Type and Format areas (Figure 10-2).

Figure 10-2: Start symbols bar.

The main difference when Mind Mapping with a pen and paper is that with MindManager there's no way of drawing branches freehand. MindManager automatically organises and positions them for you, as shown in Figure 10-3.

Figure 10-3: A formatted Mind-Manager map.

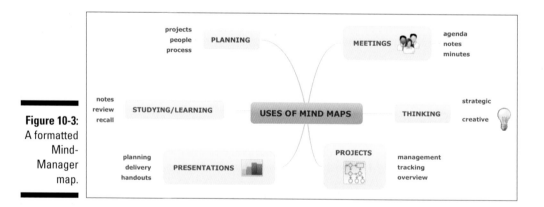

Quick notes within branches

So far I've only introduced MindManager functions which involve map displays and allow what you can also do with a pen and paper.

However, you're probably particularly interested in functions which are only possible with software and go beyond what you can achieve with a pen and paper.

Branch notes enable you to insert whole blocks of text and add pictures and tables to each branch. You can activate text notes with the [Ctrl]+[T] key combination or alternatively via the Insert symbols bar. A dialogue window (see Figure 10-4) for branch notes opens in the left or right-hand part of the screen. When you enter a note, a small note symbol appears on the branch in the Mind Map indicating that further notes are located behind it. This means that, when you minimise the branch note window again, it's still clear behind which branch further notes are located.

Using branch notes has the following advantages:

✔ You can keep your Mind Map manageable and clear and work with just one keyword per branch, yet still add further information to each branch. This is useful, for example, if you present books as Mind Maps and want to insert quotations as branch notes.

✔ You can make your Mind Map more self-explanatory by writing helpful hints in the branch memo field. It's then up to the viewer to pay attention to these branch notes or not.

✔ You can combine the clear layout of a Mind Map with the need to include continuous text. With its export function, MindManager enables you to export a Mind Map as a Word document. The individual branches are exported as headings and text notes then appear as continuous text within the Word document. This is very helpful if you use MindManager to pre-structure talks or texts.

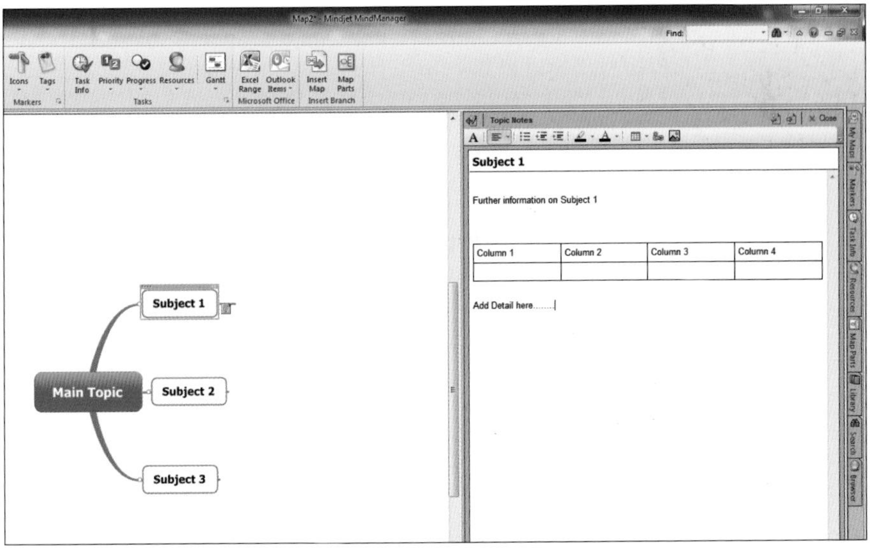

Figure 10-4:
Window
with branch
notes.

Mind Maps are essentially intended for their authors and are not self-explanatory. This is the great strength of the technique, since individual Mind Maps are memorable and quickly assimilated by the author. If you work with other people, this can be a disadvantage as you first have to explain the map concerned. Branch notes are a way of combining both strengths.

Hyperlinks – Integrating More Information into a Mind Map

Another crucial function of MindManager and Mind-Mapping software in general is the option of attaching hyperlinks to each branch. A hyperlink connects to a website or file and provides quick access to it. However, a hyperlink doesn't modify its target in any way.

MindManager allows you to attach a hyperlink to any branch and so to integrate different kinds of electronic information into a Mind Map.

The following kinds of link are provided:

- ✔ Links to internet sites starting with http://
- ✔ Links to email addresses.
- ✔ Links to individual files on your hard-disk or other drives.
- ✔ Links to particular branches in other MindManager files.
- ✔ Links to particular branches within the Mind Map concerned.
- ✔ Links to entire file folders.
- ✔ Links to Mindjet Catalyst elements. Catalyst is an additional service provided by Mindjet in return for a fee and enables joint online processing of Mind Maps over the Internet.

Just in case you feel like saying: 'So what?', let me give you a couple of examples showing how this link function is used:

- ✔ You make an internet search on a subject. You arrange your research results as a Mind Map and link each branch to the corresponding website. This means that you can go to different sites via a Mind Map.
- ✔ You use Mind Maps to prepare a text. To do this, you use a number of sources in the form of websites and pdf files. You can then connect the relevant sources via a hyperlink to the branch concerned.

✔ You use Mind Maps to structure a project. All files relating to the project, such as presentations, tables with calculations, etc., can be integrated into your Mind Map via hyperlinks, wherever these files are located on your hard-disk. It also means that you can pull together files from different folders and display them clearly in a Mind Map.

The advantage of working with hyperlinks is that you can access different information sources quickly and easily and arrange everything clearly in a Mind Map.

Inserting hyperlinks – how it works

With MindManager you can attach only one link to each branch. To do this, highlight the branch concerned and use the [Ctrl]+[K] key combination or the relevant button in the Insert symbols bar. A dialogue window then opens, as shown in Figure 10-5.

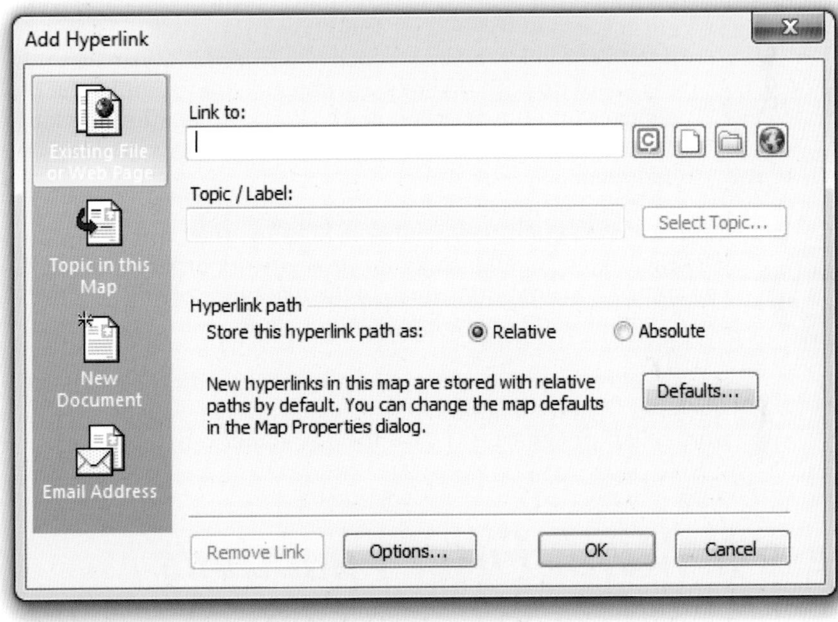

Figure 10-5:
Hyperlink
dialogue
box.

Add Hyperlink

Link to:

Topic / Label:

Select Topic...

Hyperlink path
Store this hyperlink path as: ● Relative   ○ Absolute

New hyperlinks in this map are stored with relative paths by default. You can change the map defaults in the Map Properties dialog.

Defaults...

Existing File or Web Page

Topic in this Map

New Document

Email Address

Remove Link   Options...   OK   Cancel

To the right of the line Link To there are four small buttons which you can use to activate different kinds of link. Links to websites can also be typed directly onto the lines and MindManager automatically recognises that this is an internet address.

If you insert a hyperlink to an existing file, the lower part of the dialogue box comes into play. Here you'll find two types of hyperlink:

- ✔ **Relative:** Relative in this context means that MindManager memorises the position of the link target relative to the position of the file you've opened. For example, if you've stored your file in the Work folder on your hard-drive and now link to a file located in the Work | Relocation folder, MindManager notices that your target file is in the Relocation folder and that this a sub-folder of the Work folder. If you then decide to copy your current Mind Map to another folder on your hard-drive and activate the hyperlink with this name on your Mind Map, MindManager searches for a sub-folder called Relocation from your current position and fails, since the relative structure no longer applies.

- ✔ **Absolute:** With an absolute link MindManager memorises the entire data paths of a target, for example D: | Work | Relocation | Packing List. xls. If you now move your Mind Map to another location, the functionality of your link remains unchanged, since MindManager now considers the absolute path. There's a problem if, for example, the drive letter changes and the path is now M: | Work | Relocation | Packing List.xls instead of D: | Work | Relocation | Packing List.xls, and the target can't be found.

If you want to establish a number of links to other files, for example, because you want to use MindManager for project work or knowledge management, you should consider first which of the two types of link is better suited, to avoid tedious additional work at a later stage.

I've a separate hard-drive for all data starting with the drive letter M:, even when I get a new computer. Since I can, I always use absolute links which work reliably even when I have to copy some source files.

Less Is More: Filter Functions

Another function which makes MindManager very powerful and isn't included in many Mind-Mapping programs is the filter function. This enables you to manipulate a Mind Map according to specific criteria and to display selected branches only.

MindManager provides the following filter options:

- ✔ Displaying or blanking out a selected branch.
- ✔ Displaying branches on their own without the Mind Map around them.
- ✔ Power filter: filtering according to content.

The filter functions can be accessed via the status bar and the View symbols bar (see Figure 10-6).

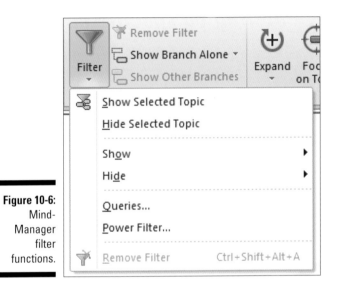

Figure 10-6:
Mind-
Manager
filter
functions.

Simple but useful: Fading branches in and out

The first two filters are easy to use and quickly described. If you highlight a particular branch you can then:

- ✔ Display this branch as the only branch of a Mind Map by clicking on Display selected branch. As soon as this filter function is activated, all other branches fade out and only the superordinate and subordinate branches remain visible. When the filter is switched on, a symbol appears in the status bar showing that a filter has been activated.

- ✔ Display this branch and its sub-branches but also cut out the higher branches and the rest of the Mind Map. If you hit the Fade in other branches, the rest of the Mind Map reappears.

Both these simple filter functions may be useful, for example, if:

- ✔ A Mind Map has become so complex that clarity is impaired.
- ✔ You want to print out just selected parts of a map. You can filter several times until only those branches that you want to print remain.
- ✔ You want to show a Mind Map to someone else but would like to select only certain parts of it.

Power filter: Filtering by specific criteria

As its name suggests, the power filter (shown in Figure 10-7) is a more powerful tool.

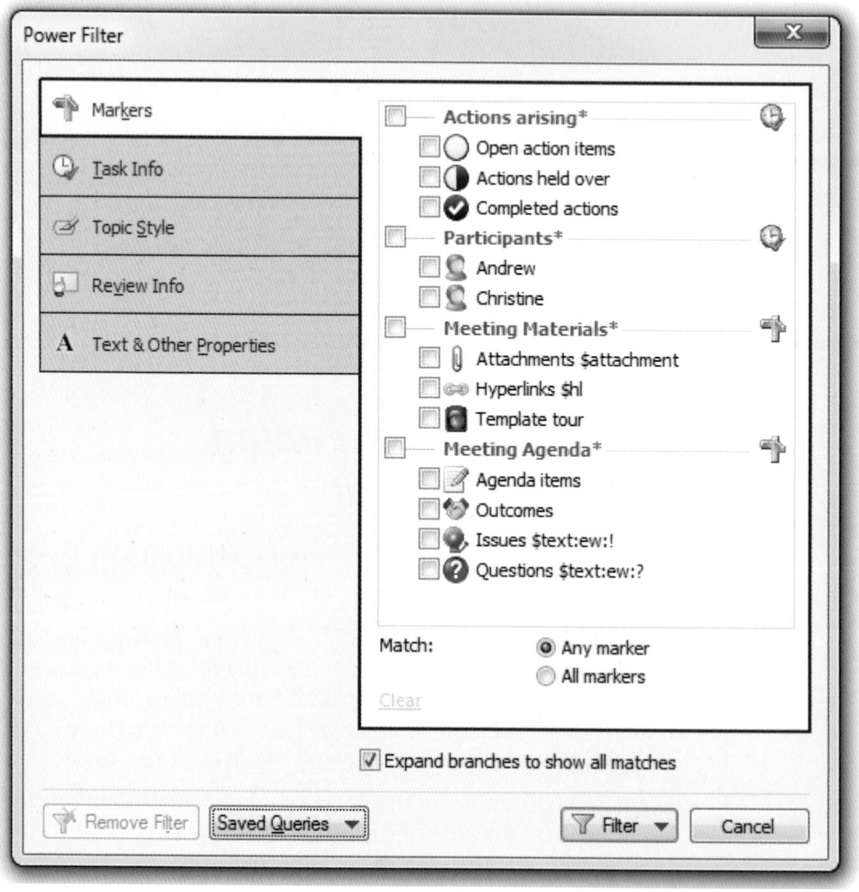

Figure 10-7:
Power filter
dialogue
box in Mind-
Manager.

The power filter allows you to filter information in a Mind Map according to different criteria.

These are:

- **Highlighting:** You can filter with the icons provided by MindManager. If you activate the power filter function, all icons currently being used in the Mind Map are displayed in the Highlighting tab. For example, you can display or fade out any branches containing the exclamation mark symbol (see Figure 10-7).

- **Task info:** You can assign relevant data like start date, end date and task priority to each branch for project management via the Task info tab. You can then filter the assigned data in the power filter dialogue box via the Task info tab. For example, you can display all branches to be actioned by the end of the week.

- **Branch style:** This function enables you to filter different branch templates from the template store.

- **Revision info:** Just like Microsoft Word, MindManager has a revision function which you can use to trace alterations. You can use the power filter to search through all changes and branch comments, for example, so as to display any branches that have been altered by a colleague.

- **Text and other properties:** Branches can contain additional elements like the branch notes or hyperlinks described above. You can use the power function to display or fade out branches with features that are useful for you.

The Highlighting and Text and other properties tabs in the power filter contain a field called Compliance with the options: One property and All properties. This constitutes an And/Or distinction. For example, if you select several icons simultaneously under Highlighting and then click on All properties, only those branches are displayed that simultaneously have all the icons you selected.

MindManager's power filter means that the symbols used in Mind Maps also acquire a filter criterion function in addition to being quick and easy to view. Hence, with the power filter you can make a suitable selection for your present information requirements in just a few seconds and, for example, filter by priority, due date or attachment.

Project Management with GANTT Diagrams

Project management with GANTT diagrams was previously available only as an expensive add-on but is now included in MindManager as standard. The GANTT button in the View symbols bar allows you to display all branches along a timeline in the form of a GANTT diagram (see Figure 10-8).

This display contains only those branches to which you've previously assigned further details in the Task info tab in the Task Pane.

In addition to the branch name and start and end date, progress status is also marked here in colour (see Figure 10-8).

As with other project-management programs, you can alter start and end times for individual branches by moving the bar inside the GANTT display. Hence, MindManager makes scheduling a Mind-Map-type project easy for you.

Adding task information to branches

For the MindManager's GANTT functions to work, you must have previously added task information to the branches concerned. This is done with the Task info tab in the Work maps register (see Figure 10-9). This tab provides detailed information on the highlighted branch and allows you to make changes. You can then make a power filter search of the information you enter there. Thus, for example, you can search a Mind Map for people you've defined as a resource and clearly display all the tasks of a particular individual.

You can establish how one branch depends on another in terms of their respective timeframes and show these dependences in the GANTT display. To do this, activate the field, scroll through task info to this point for each branch in the Task info tab under Task management. You can then establish the time dependencies between two branches, for example, End-start, meaning that task B should start before task A has ended. MindManager adjusts the times for task B accordingly.

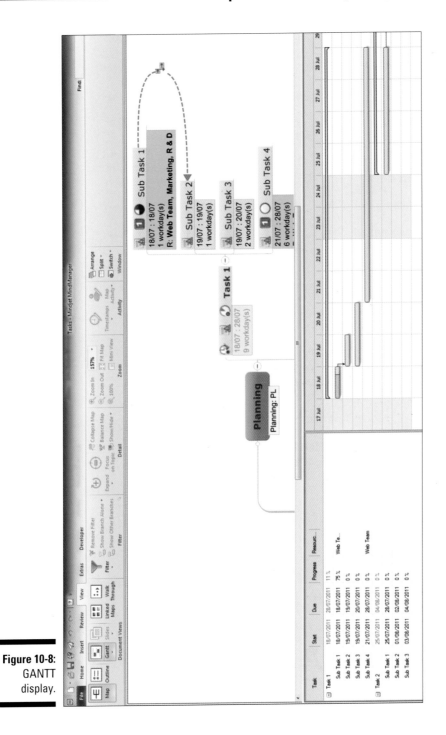

Figure 10-8:
GANTT
display.

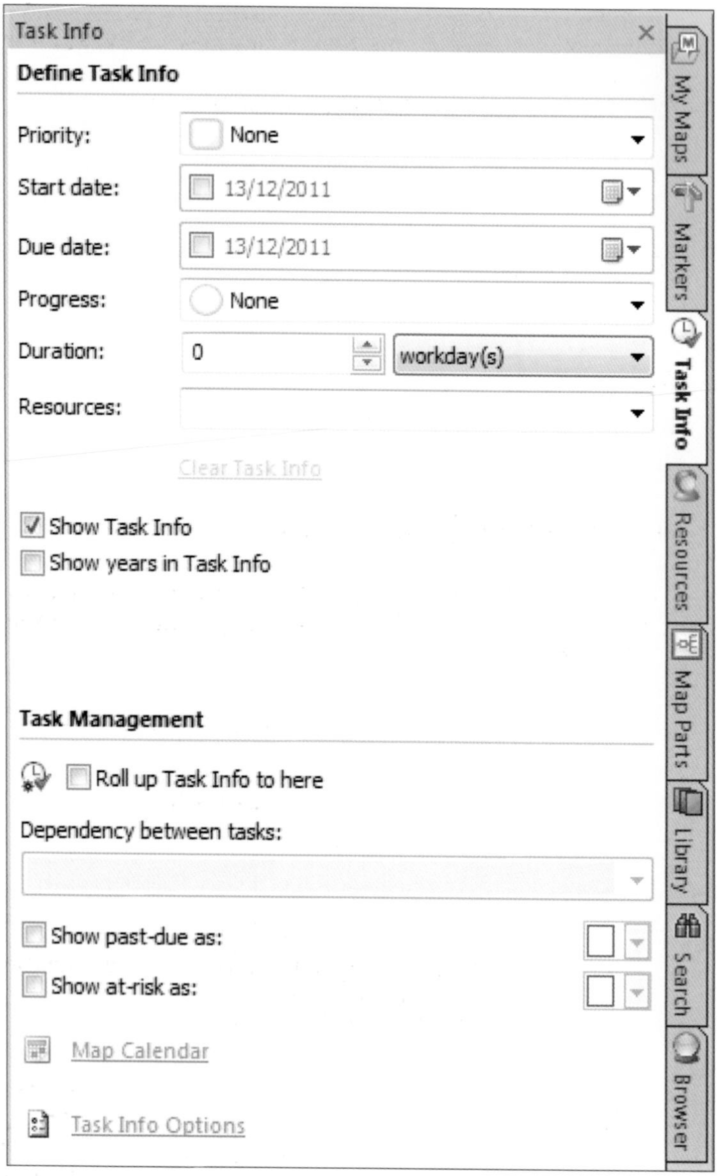

Figure 10-9:
Defining
task
information.

Exporting and Processing

Sometimes it's not enough simply to have access to your Mind Map in a
Mind-Mapping program only. MindMapping includes a number of export

functions which allow you to share a Mind Map with other people and/or make it available in other formats. You need the Export symbols bar for this.

I now examine the following export options more closely:

- ✔ Enable
- ✔ Export as Mindjet Player
- ✔ pdf
- ✔ Export as an image
- ✔ Pack&Go
- ✔ Word
- ✔ PowerPoint

Sharing your Mind Map

Among many other things, you can automatically send an email to someone with a link to your Mind Map. This function is provided by the Mindjet-Catalyst platform (see Figure 10-10).

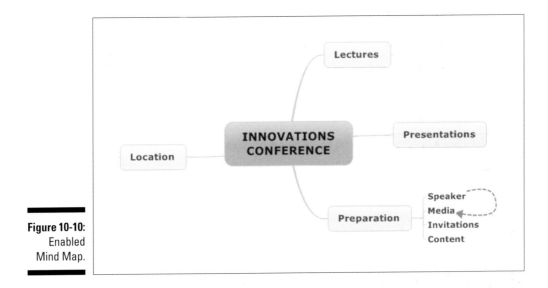

Figure 10-10:
Enabled
Mind Map.

The other person can now navigate through a copy of your Mind Map online but is unable to edit it. To do that would require the Mindjet-Catalyst service, available in return for a fee.

Mindjet Player – interactive pdf document

With Mindjet Player you can equip a pdf document with the interactive functions described above and then email it. Unlike an ordinary pdf document, a Mindjet Player document is interactive. As shown in Figure 10-10, you can click on a Mind Map under construction in a pdf document. You should have a current version of Adobe Reader to be able to display these pdf documents.

pdf – easy and practical

In a time of sophisticated IT security measures in businesses it's not so easy to provide content in a way that can be readily opened. Many options are deactivated by security settings.

Exporting a Mind Map as a pdf file is guaranteed to work. The Mind Map is integrated into a pdf file as an image in landscape format. This option is quick, easy and particularly suitable if you only want your Mind Map to be displayed.

Image files for integration into other documents

Image file exporting is ultimately the same as pdf exporting, but in a different format. The advantage of this is that you can incorporate the image file into other documents, for example, a presentation or as a picture on a website.

Pack&Go – and all the links work

Pack&Go is aimed at two target persons: you yourself and other MindManager users.

The Pack&Go function provides you with a MindManager file and other documents in a .zip-file which can be opened on another computer with MindManager installed on it. Particularly useful is the fact that Pack&Go also allows you to package documents to which you've linked your Mind Map in the .zip-file and to adapt the link structure to make all documents available to another computer and open them there. Hence the name Pack&Go.

You can decide in advance which of the documents linked to your Mind Map you wish to package.

Word – presenting a Mind Map as a linear document

Using Word export you can convert a Mind Map and elements like branch notes into a text document. This abandons the graphic form of the Mind Map and presents content as a linear sequence of information just like in this book.

MindManager can convert Mind-Map content in formatted form into a text, for example, by numbering the branch levels and inserting them as headings in the Word document. You can decide and determine in detail which elements of your Mind Map you wish to export (see Figure 10-11).

The function is useful if you use Mind Maps as a way of pre-structuring and preparing texts, for example, the minutes of meetings or texts. Notes added to a branch then appear in the Word document as continuous text beneath a numbered heading.

PowerPoint – from branches to bullet points

The famous (or infamous) PowerPoint presentations are ubiquitous and so MindManager also offers the means of breaking up a Mind Map into this format.

In this way, the Mind Map is literally broken up into small morsels and transferred to transparencies or slides. Each main branch on level 1 is displayed as a heading on a transparency. Any sub-branches appear as bullet points and dashes.

This function too may be useful if you have to transfer a Mind Map to linear format.

When a Mind Map is converted to linear format a lot of its information content is lost. A combination of both may be useful. A Mind Map can be inserted as an image file into a presentation file to give viewers an idea of the connections within the Mind Map. Detailed information can then be displayed in the ordinary presentation form.

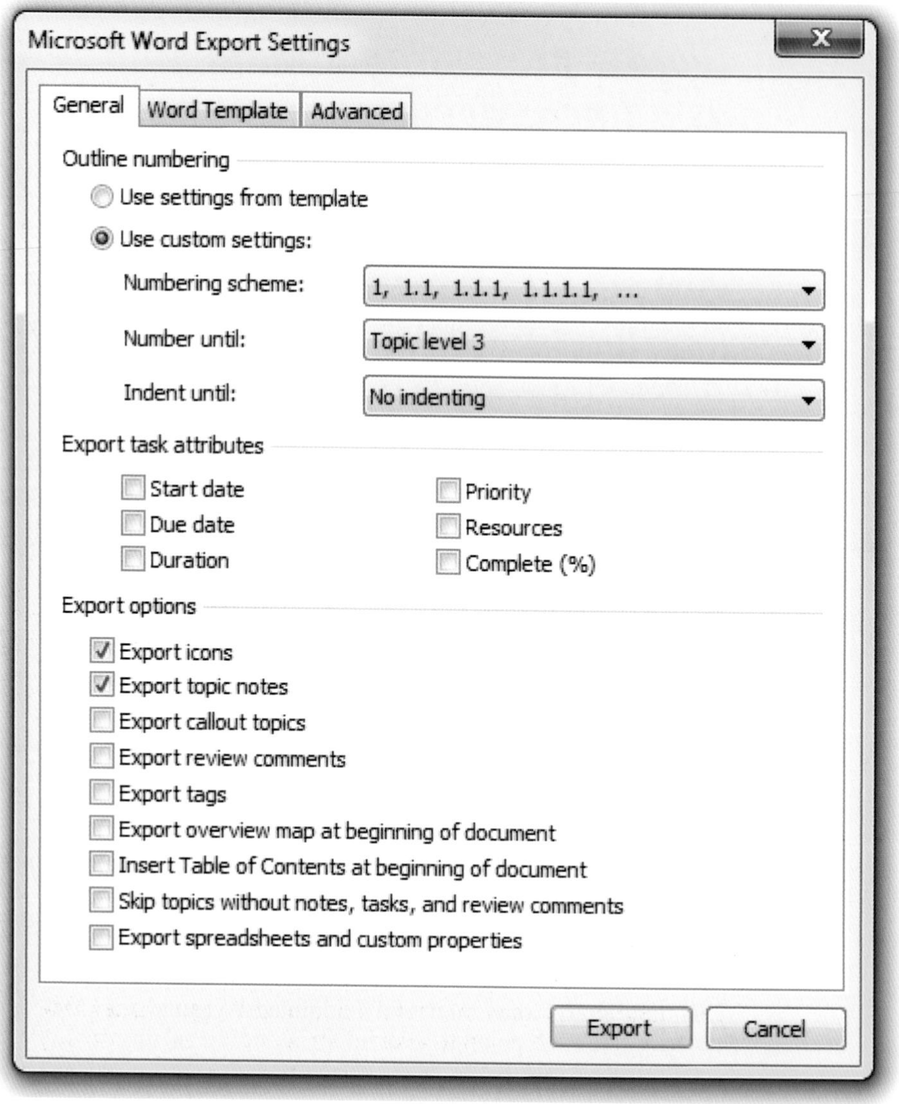

Microsoft Word Export Settings   ✕

| General | Word Template | Advanced |

Outline numbering

  ○ Use settings from template

  ◉ Use custom settings:

    Numbering scheme: 1, 1.1, 1.1.1, 1.1.1.1, ... ▼

    Number until: Topic level 3 ▼

    Indent until: No indenting ▼

Export task attributes

  ☐ Start date   ☐ Priority

  ☐ Due date   ☐ Resources

  ☐ Duration   ☐ Complete (%)

Export options

  ☑ Export icons

  ☑ Export topic notes

  ☐ Export callout topics

  ☐ Export review comments

  ☐ Export tags

  ☐ Export overview map at beginning of document

  ☐ Insert Table of Contents at beginning of document

  ☐ Skip topics without notes, tasks, and review comments

  ☐ Export spreadsheets and custom properties

[Export] [Cancel]

Figure 10-11:
Word
export.

Presentation Mode: From Mind Map to Presentation in a Single Click

A very useful feature is MindManager's presentation mode. This can be found in the View symbols bar, as shown in Figure 10-12.

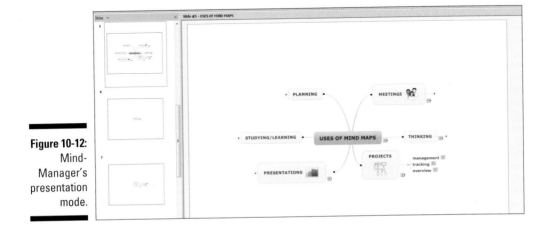

Figure 10-12:
Mind-
Manager's
presentation
mode.

Presentation mode allows you to present a Mind Map to an audience in small pieces. If you activate presentation mode, only the central theme and the main branches are displayed. Using the Further key the lecturer can present the Mind Map to the audience bit by bit and take the viewers through its content stage by stage. You can determine in advance how the Mind Map will be presented, for example, whether open branches should stay open or be closed after you have discussed them.

Presentation mode has a number of advantages which make it very attractive:

✔ With just the press of a key you can jump from your Mind-Map notes to a presentation: this means you save a lot of time that you'd normally spend on setting up presentations.

✔ Your audience sees the full extent of the Mind Map at all times and can understand its connections and, in addition, you can fade in just single aspects of the map to avoid distracting or overburdening your viewers.

- ✔ Presentation mode enables you to work on the Mind Map while it's being presented. This means you can make presentations even more interactive.

- ✔ MindManager includes many pictures and symbols which make Mind Maps visually pleasing and appealing.

- ✔ Content that's hard to present in a Mind Map, such as tables, can be integrated in the form of links and activated with the touch of a key during the presentation.

As this kind of presentation is still not very widespread, you'll definitely surprise your audience. I've had very positive experiences with it so far.

Chapter 11

Exploring ThinkBuzan's iMindMap

*T*hinkBuzan's iMindMap is a great software program:

- ✔ iMindMap is one of the few programs that enable you to generate, among other things, so-called organic Mind Maps based on the appearance of traditional Mind Maps drawn with a pen and paper.

- ✔ iMindMap was developed by the inventor of Mind Maps, Tony Buzan, and successfully transfers the principles of the Mind-Mapping technique to the computer.

- ✔ iMindMap differs from most other Mind-Mapping programs in its appearance and use. It's very simple and clear and gives the user the impression that they are actually drawing a Mind Map and not using software.

- ✔ Run on a tablet PC, iMindMap enables you to generate Mind Maps by hand or with a special stylus developed for tablet PCs. This replicates the sensory experience of drawing a map and resembles it very closely. The package is also available from iTunes as apps for Apple iPad and Apple iPhones.

 The sensory experience of writing and drawing by hand has important psychological effects that are lost when using software. If you want to use Mind Maps for learning, memorising and preparing for exams, Mind Maps which you have drawn yourself are more easily assimilated and retained.

In this chapter we focus on iMindMap 5, which is available in three versions: Basic, Home & Students and Ultimate, with the number of functions and price increasing in that order. In this chapter I'm working with the Ultimate version of the package.

- **iMindMap Basic** (free) provides standard functions for generating Mind Maps and, according to the manufacturer, is especially suitable for private users and students.

- **Home & Student** ($39.00/€49.00/$67.00) has additional export functions, SmartLayout, Custom Styling, Multi Maps and the option of altering the view of a Mind Map, for example, by expanding and collapsing branches.

- **The Ultimate version** ($149.00/€190.00/$256.00) also contains project management functions, 3D Mind Map View, full export options, a presentation mode, ability to insert flowcharts and spreadsheets, and integration with Microsoft and Open-Office programs.

If you're the proud owner of a tablet PC, that is, a laptop that in addition to a keyboard and touchpad can be controlled directly via a touch screen, then you should certainly give iMindMap a try. With a tablet PC you can draw with a stylus directly on the screen, rather like with a pen and paper. The program even has a signature recognition function. In this way you can combine the advantages of a computer with the tactile experience of pen and paper.

There are also iMindMap versions for iPhone and iPad. Writing is entered with the virtual keypad.

Basic Use – Finding Your Way Around

iMindMap is clearly laid out and easy to use as you can see in Figure 11-1. Basic operation is quickly mastered.

I'd like to highlight the following functions:

- **Map area:** As with MindManager this takes up most of the screen. It's where you draw your maps.

- **Tool bar:** iMindMap has only one symbols bar and a side panel in addition to buttons like View, Insert and Format.

- **Formatting bar:** This is located in the toolbar and contains options for formatting the branches of the Mind Map you have made.

- **Side panel:** You can activate functions like the icon library or the pictures library from the side panel on the right of the screen.

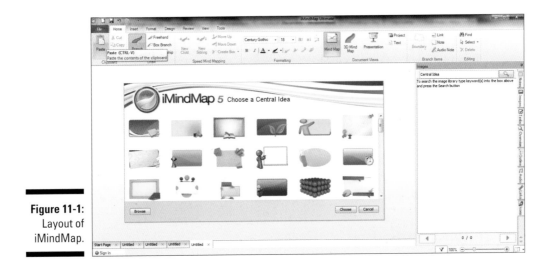

Figure 11-1:
Layout of
iMindMap.

Branches

With iMindMap you can generate organic Mind Maps, meaning they look like they've been drawn with a pen and paper, or a more linear, straight branching style. You can also decide how long branches should be and in which directions they should point. Branches are mainly added with the mouse. For rapid entry of large amounts of information in iMindMap there is the *Speed Mind Mapping mode* which I shall be presenting a little later in this chapter.

Adding branches

To add a branch:

1. Hover the mouse across your central idea or the end of an existing branch so that a red dot appears.

2. From this red dot, you can now add a branch by clicking, dragging out and releasing.

This procedure applies to both the central idea and to any branch. As soon as you move the mouse cursor to the end of a branch, a red dot and a blue circle appear (see Figure 11-2).

You can add new branches by moving the red dot. By moving the blue cross you can alter the position, direction and length of an existing branch.

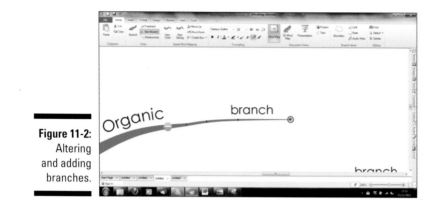

Figure 11-2:
Altering
and adding
branches.

Altering the shape of branches

In addition to the length and direction of individual branches you can also manually change their shape. To do this, highlight a branch by clicking on it with the mouse. Small blue dots called 'control points' then appear along the branch. By moving these dots around you can alter the shape of branches (see Figure 11-3).

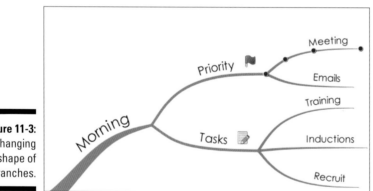

Figure 11-3:
Changing
the shape of
branches.

Adding text to a branch

To add text, highlight the branch concerned and type it in directly. If you highlight a branch that has text on it, new text can be typed in and added to the words already there.

Three kinds of branch

If you click on Draw in the symbols bar, you will notice that iMindMap distinguishes between three kinds of branch, shown in Figure 11-4:

- ✔ **Organic branches:** These look like they've been drawn by hand, but iMindMap helps you with positioning the branches.

- ✔ **Freehand branches:** You're completely free to determine the shape of branches, just as you'd draw them with a stylus on the screen. iMindMap doesn't provide support here but allows you complete creative freedom.

- ✔ **Box branches:** These let you write several lines of sentences on a branch. Information is placed in a text box. Clearly the designers of iMindMap realised that many software users don't stick to the one-word rule but want to use more than one keyword per branch. This is possible with box branches.

Although you should only insert one word per branch when Mind Mapping, text-field branches can be useful, for example, for quotations or inserting larger chunks of text.

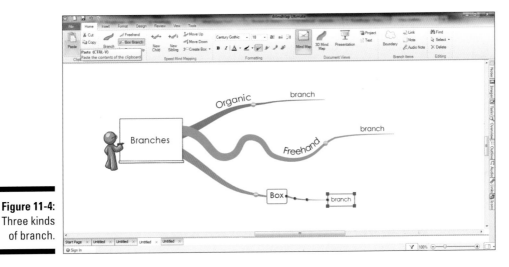

Figure 11-4:
Three kinds
of branch.

Two Input Methods: Mind Mapping and Speed Mind Mapping

iMindMap enables you to design and draw Mind Maps freely, just like with a pen and paper. It allows you to 'draw' branches with the mouse. The advantage of this is that you can organise branches just how you like. However, by doing so you sacrifice speed. Therefore, iMindMap contains two different input methods:

✔ **Mind Mapping:** This is the standard method. It's used for inputting information in the way I describe above. You'll probably use this method most of the time when running iMindMap.

✔ **Speed Mind Mapping:** This input method is specially designed for quickly inputting a lot of data via the keyboard in a short time. iMindMap's SmartLayout controls the map's layout.

Speed Mind Mapping – how it works

iMindMap's Speed Mind Mapping mode functions with the same keys as those used with MindManager:

✔ **Enter key:** Adds a new branch on the same level. For example, if you're at main-branch level, then another main branch is added. As soon as the branch appears, you can type your text onto it. When you've finished, click on [Enter] again.

✔ **Tab:** Insert a new branch at a deeper level. So, if you're at main-branch level again and press [Tab], a new sub-branch is generated next to the main branch highlighted by you.

✔ **Backspace:** Pressing this key deletes the highlighted branch and all its sub-branches.

Formatting with iMindMap

iMindMap offers you other options in addition to freely organising branches. Via the formatting bar you can set basic features like branch colour, script colour and script size for each branch.

Moreover, iMindMap provides a range of further options for the visual presentation of Mind Maps:

✔ **Icon library:** You can access over 100 icons of different types. You can add as many as you like to each branch. You can also filter icons.

✔ **Image library:** Via its image library and an online link iMindMap provides access to thousands of images which can be searched through by keyword. The search function works best with English keywords. Mindjet MindManager provides a limited number of rather stylised graphics, whereas iMindMap offers access to a virtually unlimited number of, unfortunately, not particularly attractive pictures.

✔ **Image files:** With iMindMap you can incorporate any image files, for example company logos, in your Mind Map.

✔ **Relationship arrows:** Just as with a pen and paper, with iMindMap you can add relationship arrows between two branches via the Draw menu.

✔ **Boundaries:** By means of the Insert⎮Boundary menu you can add a border to a highlighted branch. You can alter the cloud settings to a certain extent by selecting Boundary from the Format menu (see Figure 11-5).

✔ **Drawing:** By clicking on Add⎮Drawing you can access a rudimentary drawing program with which you can generate graphics and then add them to your Mind Map (see Figure 11-6). This is particularly relevant for users of tablet PCs, as you can draw by using the stylus.

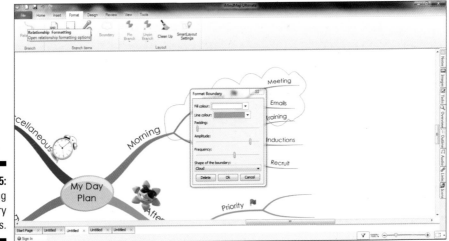

Figure 11-5:
Adjusting
Boundary
settings.

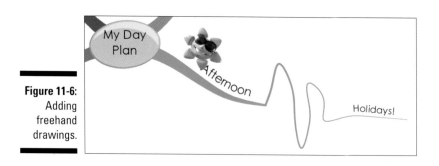

Figure 11-6:
Adding
freehand
drawings.

SmartLayout: From linear to radial Mind Maps

An interesting function offered only by iMindMap in this form is the
SmartLayout function, which is automatic. You can change SmartLayout settings or turn them off by selecting SmartLayout from the Format menu.

As the name suggests, iMindMap takes over the organisation and arrangement of branches with this. However, as the user you've a choice of different
layout variants between which you can switch (see Figure 11-7).

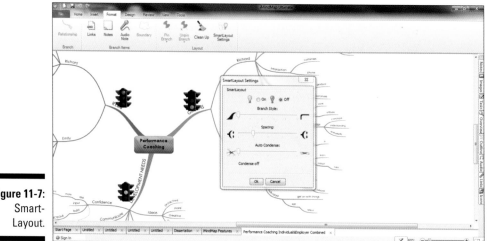

Figure 11-7:
Smart-
Layout.

iMindMap enables you to choose your own options:

 ✔ **Linear:** This involves the 'fish-bone' design familiar from many other
   programs (see Figure 11-8).

✔ **Organic:** This layout looks more natural and as if drawn by hand. The Mind Maps displayed so far in this chapter use organic layout.

✔ **Radial:** This setting allows you to arrange the branches of a Mind Map so they point outwards from its centre, just like spokes radiating from the centre of a circle (see Figure 11-9).

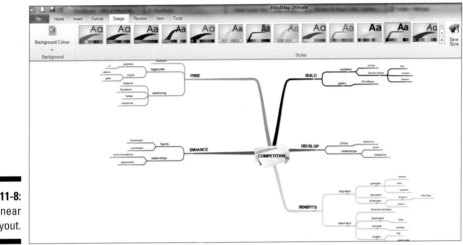

Figure 11-8:
Linear
layout.

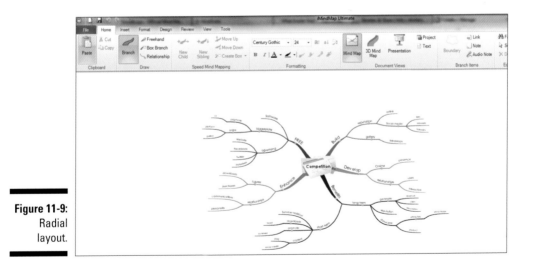

Figure 11-9:
Radial
layout.

This function enables you to modify the appearance of your Mind Map in any way you like.

Further properties of branches

Like MindManager, iMindMap can do more than just generate displays. Each branch can be equipped by using a number of additional functionalities:

- ✔ **Hyperlinks:** Each branch can contain as many links as you like, either to files or to web addresses. The hyperlink function is accessed via the Insert function.

- ✔ **Notes:** A text window can be opened for each branch via the Notesfunction. In this way you can add as much continuous text and as many tables and images as you like. Hence, iMindMap enables you to generate Mind Maps with one word per branch and yet to add additional information to each branch.

- ✔ **Audio notes:** Only iMindMap has this function. You can add audio notes to any branch. For example, you can present a Mind Map to a colleague with branches that speak a couple of sentences!

Project-management mode: GANTT view

Like MindManager, iMindMap also has a project-management mode, accessed via the Project button. You can then enter data to assist with project management:

- ✔ Start date
- ✔ End date
- ✔ Progress status
- ✔ Priority
- ✔ Resources

Data attached to each branch can be displayed for ready reference in the form of a GANTT diagram (see Figure 11-10).

iMindMap then isn't a replacement for project-management software, such as that required for more complicated projects. But the program is quite adequate for many small projects, it's easy to use and both a Mind Map and time sequence can be viewed at the same time.

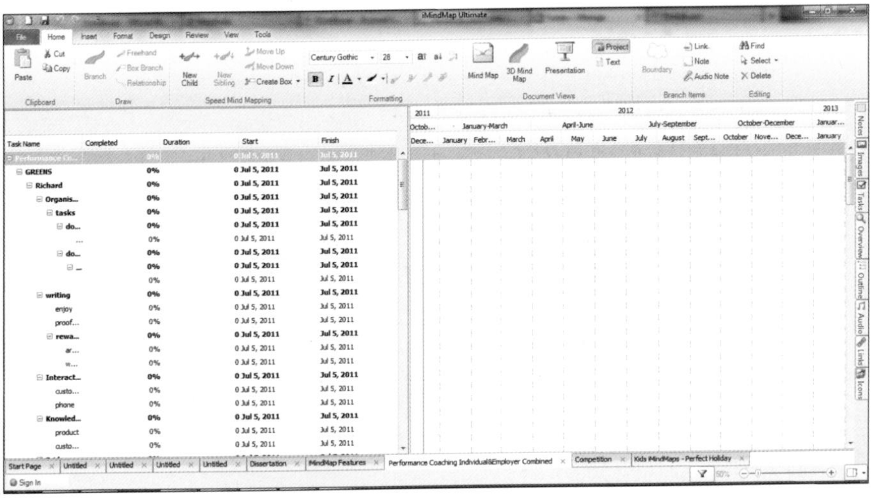

Figure 11-10:
Project
management
mode.

Project Management with iMindMap, Step by Step

Here's a step-by-step account of project management with iMindMap.

Step 1: Select the branches concerned

If you switch to Project View in any Mind Map, a GANTT diagram appears in place of your Mind Map.

iMindMap automatically sets all added branches of a Mind Map to project-management mode. However, in my experience not all branches need to be loaded with data and resources but only with selected elements.

The Tasks side panel (Figure 11-11) contains all the setting options of a branch for project management. At the bottom of the Tasks side panel you can 'Enable for Project Management'. If you uncheck the box, the branch disappears from the list of branches activated for project management. In an admittedly somewhat impractical way you then have to deactivate all the branches which you don't want to include in project-management mode.

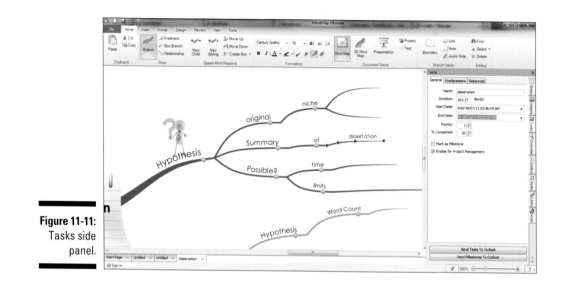

Figure 11-11:
Tasks side
panel.

Step 2: Inputting task details

Now that only those branches you really want to work with remain, you can input task details on each branch. To do this, open the Tasks side panel and select the branch you wish to input task details for. This allows you to enter the following settings:

- **Input the start and end date.** As soon as the start and end date have been entered, iMindMap will calculate the time in days.

- **Set the start and end time.**

- **Assign priority.**

- **Indicate progress status as a percentage.** You can enter progress status either directly here via the menu or simply by clicking on the cross symbol which appears on every branch in project- management mode.

- **Assign resources.** Here, for example, you can add personal names to a branch. Before you can add resources, you must first hit the Manage button. They then appear in the options bar.

- **Set superordinate branches or Predecessors.** This function is only relevant to the view in the GANTT diagram. Here you can indicate whether any other task of your project has to be completed first, before the present task can be carried out (see Figure 11-12).

When you've entered your instructions, the view in the GANTT diagram will change accordingly.

Step 3: Adjusting views

Now all tasks have been entered. In the project-management window you'll see on the left-hand side a table summarising all branches concerned. The GANTT diagram is displayed on the right-hand side. The distribution of both windows can be adjusted so that, for example, you can create more space for the diagram. At the top of the diagram you can choose from various time intervals in which the diagram will be presented. This is helpful for switching between the overview and details.

Presenting the Mind Map

As with MindManager, iMindMap allows you to present your Mind Maps. In addition to having an integrated presentation mode, PowerPoint fans can also get value for money here.

Really quite presentable: Presentation mode

iMindMap includes a presentation mode which is fun to use. By using the presentation mode you can take an audience through a Mind Map step by step (see Figure 11-13). A new branch is superimposed with each press of the key. You also have the option to present your Mind Maps in 3D View, which is visually stimulating for your audience.

Unlike MindManager, with iMindMap you can't skip individual branches or edit the Mind Map during presentation. Moreover, if the presentation mode is switched off for a while, iMindMap doesn't allow you to return to a particular place in the presentation, like you can with PowerPoint. You have to click through the whole Mind Map every time.

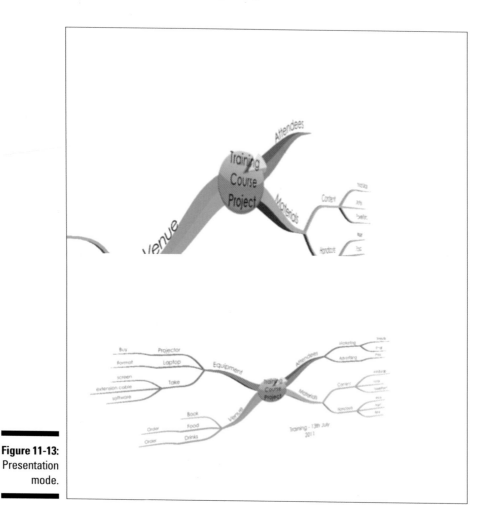

Figure 11-13:
Presentation
mode.

Nevertheless, the presentation mode is an attractive way of presenting a generated Mind Map to an audience step by step.

An alternative: Exporting as a PowerPoint presentation

What's really impressive and a good alternative to presentation mode is exporting a Mind Map as an *interactive presentation*. This means that the Mind Map is integrated into a PowerPoint file. Each branch is exported as an autonomous graphic and superimposed on the screen one after the other via the user-defined PowerPoint animation (see Figure 11-14). Thus, the entire Mind Map appears in a single transparency and is built up in many individual steps.

In this way the Mind-Map presentation can become part of a PowerPoint presentation which, in addition to the Mind Map, can contain other transparencies as well.

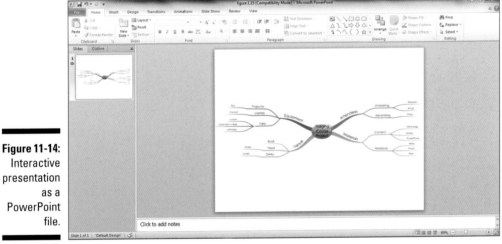

Figure 11-14:
Interactive presentation as a PowerPoint file.

If you like hand-drawn Mind Maps, then iMindMap should be the package of choice. Also important is iMindMap's user-friendliness, with the techniques being mastered in just a few hours.

Part IV
Advanced Strategies for Mind Mapping

The 5th Wave — By Rich Tennant

"Okay – let's try brainstorming again, only this time with a little less storm."

In this part . . .

With your grounding in the basics and an overview of Mind Mapping software, you're now ready to tackle advanced Mind Mapping applications.

In this part you learn how to read textbooks quickly and efficiently and to deal with Mind Map notes. I show you how you can tackle projects and knowledge management with Mind Mapping software.

Lastly, I cover how you can use Mind Mapping systematically in creative problem solving.

Chapter 12

Mind Mapping Reading Techniques

● ●

In This Chapter

▶ The kinds of books you can work on with Mind Maps

▶ A reading method in four stages

▶ Making records from different textual sources

● ●

Maybe you're already familiar with the following situations:

✔ You're reading an interesting textbook. Unfortunately, by the time you reach the end and put the book back on the shelf, you've already forgotten most of its content and interesting details.

✔ You have to read and understand books or large texts for your job and would like to have your questions answered by the book as quickly as possible.

In this chapter I introduce you to a special procedure which combines Mind Mapping with aspects of fast-reading techniques so that you can understand and retain a lot of information in as short a time as possible. This procedure is particularly sensible for specialist texts or textbooks whose content you wish to assimilate, for example, because you'll need to refer to it again later or because you want to prepare for exams.

The main features of this approach are:

✔ You use the 80/20 rule or so-called Pareto principle. In simple terms this states that 80 per cent of results are achieved within 20 per cent of a project's total time. The remaining 20 per cent of results take up most of the time.

✔ The aim of the technique is to ensure that working through textbooks is as economical as possible. So, you try to achieve the best possible result as quickly as possible in the time allowed, that is, understanding and assimilating as much of a book as possible. To work through a book in its entirety and retain every last detail would take up much too much time (80 per cent according to the Pareto principle), so you limit yourself to what's essential.

✔ You not only read a book from cover to cover but also passages within it. In each passage you concentrate on specific aspects. You read as few passages as possible but as many as you need. This will take less time than if you just read the book from A to Z.

This approach is not intended for novels read for pleasure. In that case you want to enjoy an exciting story and not spoil the suspense by starting a crime story in the last chapter and finding out in advance who the murderer is.

The technique is divided into two parts:

✔ Preparation before actually starting to read

✔ The reading process itself

Appreciating the Fine Art of Preparation

Preparation is especially sensible for long texts like books. The time you invest in preparation will pay dividends at the subsequent reading stage.

Preparation can itself be subdivided into three steps:

1. Skimming the text

2. Recalling background knowledge

3. Setting questions and aims

Step 1: Skimming the text

The first step involves skimming the text. The aim is to get a basic impression and general overview of the book's structure. When skimming a book you don't actually read but look at each page for just a couple of seconds.

1. **Get an initial impression.** Two things happen when you skim: you gain a first impression and get some idea of the difficulty and structure of the book. For example, you find out whether the author includes introductions and summaries, uses illustrations and graphics or focuses mainly on text.

2. **Prioritise.** This may help you to determine which sections you actually need to read and which ones you can omit or pay less attention to. In the case of textbooks it's extremely rare that you need to read absolutely everything.

Step 2: Recalling background knowledge

You may often read textbooks on subjects you already know something about or have already worked on in the past. It's rarely the case that you know absolutely nothing about the subject concerned.

You should try to recall this background knowledge in these two preparatory steps. The aim is to put your thoughts and knowledge of the subject down on paper and to reactivate your knowledge in this way. This will make reading the book and establishing new mental connections easier. It goes without saying that you can use a Mind Map when putting this material on paper.

So, take a fresh sheet of paper and marshal your thoughts in a Mind Map, just like I demonstrate in Chapter 5.

You don't need to produce a perfectly structured Mind Map on your topic at this stage. So, don't worry too much about its precise structure but try to recall what knowledge you have and put it down quickly onto paper or screen.

Step 3: Setting questions and aims

Before starting to read, you need to set as many specific questions and aims as possible: ask yourself what the aim of reading the textbook actually is. Consider whether there are specific questions you'd like to address.

If you read a book about trend forecasting, for example, your aim may be to get to know the most important methods used by trend forecasters and be able to describe them.

If you're a school pupil or student, you'll often be given specific questions by your teacher or tutor and have to answer them after reading a book. For example: 'According to theory XY, what are the main factors that explain how financial crises occur?'.

You should write down these questions and aims and keep them to hand when reading. Questions and aims are a sort of filter that help you focus your attention during reading and know what you should bear in mind. They'll also help you to take more targeted notes.

Of course, it may be that your aim is simply to read the whole book and understand its content. But even then it's useful to have come up with specific questions which you can answer.

Honing the Reading Process

Now you can actually start to read. The technique is designed rather like a Russian matryoshka doll – you read the text from the outside inwards. Depending on the text and reading aim, you can use the entire procedure or just the first couple of steps.

The reading process set out below also requires you to take notes in Mind-Map form, as demonstrated in Chapter 7.

You shouldn't try to cram everything into a single Mind Map. Create as many Mind Maps as you need to organise what in your view is the most important content.

This reading procedure can be broken down into four steps:

1. Skim reading
2. Preview
3. Immersion
4. Difficult passages

We'll now take a closer look at these steps together.

Step 1: Skim reading

In your first read-through read the:

- ✔ Introductions
- ✔ Summaries
- ✔ Headings and subheadings
- ✔ Tables and illustrations

As you read, transfer the material gleaned from these sections into your Mind Map. This procedure can be applied to the whole book. If the book has a section headed 'Introduction' and one headed 'Summary/Conclusion', then read these two sections first of all.

You can then apply the same method to these sections and check, for example, whether the section 'Introduction' itself has introductions, summaries, headings, subheadings, and so on.

When you've read the 'Introduction' and 'Summary' sections, move on to the main chapters in similar fashion and add material to your Mind Map or extend it accordingly.

It's often the case that an introduction and summary already contain much of the information set out in the chapters. It may be that the information in these two sections is sufficient for you to answer your questions and achieve your targets. If so, you can then lay the book aside. There's no reason why you should spend any more time on it. If you haven't achieved your aims, then in any case skim reading will make further reading easier, since you now have an idea of how the remaining chapters or the whole book are laid out.

Step 2: Preview

Depending on the book's layout, in this step you read the first and last paragraphs of each section of a chapter and add any extracted material to your Mind Map. There's no fixed procedure here. It also depends to a certain extent on the kind of book and its layout. It's sometimes useful to read the first and last paragraphs and can occasionally be helpful to read the first and last sentences of each paragraph too.

Step 3: Immersion

If you still haven't achieved your reading targets, now read all paragraphs in detail and extend your Mind Map with new material you consider important. Particularly difficult passages that you don't understand even after several readings can be put on hold for now and marked accordingly. You can return to these passages when you've reached the end. Their meaning may become clearer as you progress through the book.

Step 4: Difficult passages

In the last step you focus your attention on the difficult passages you've already marked as such. The Mind Map you've been preparing so far may help you to elucidate their meaning in light of the book as a whole. Any new information gleaned in this way can also be entered in the existing Mind Map.

Figure 12-1 illustrates how the Mind Map you use to make notes grows step by step.

The reading technique presented here is similar to the procedure used for generating a Mind Map. In step 1 you are at main-branch level and insert the first details into the map. In steps 2 to 4 you work through the substance of the book and can add relevant sub-branches to your Mind Map. The fact that you can extend and supplement Mind Maps flexibly at any time is particularly well suited to this kind of modular reading. Having a constant overview of everything (the Mind Map) and previous knowledge about the text make reading much easier.

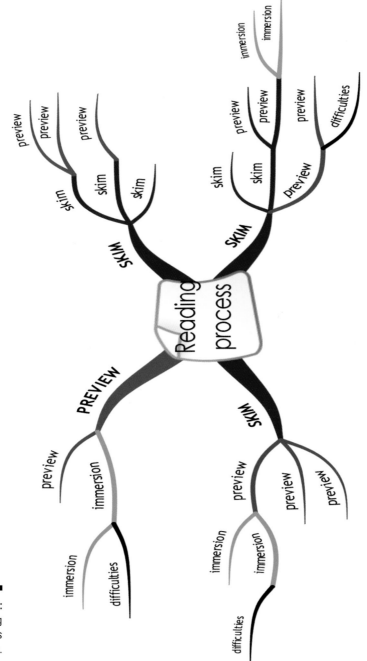

Figure 12-1:
The reading
process as
a Mind Map.

Figure 12-2 summarises again the main points of the reading technique presented in this chapter in the form of a Mind Map:

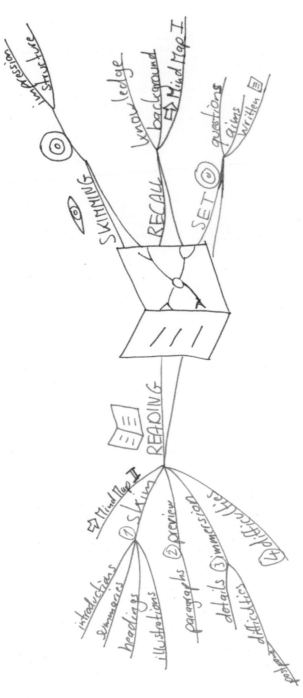

Figure 12-2:
Overview of
the reading
technique.

In Chapter 7, I introduced the 'just write it down' technique. This technique involves not only fixing information you have gathered, that is, heard or read, but also your own thoughts which are not in the book but are connected with the subject concerned. It's a good idea to reserve a particular colour to be used for your thoughts on the topic. You can enter these into your Mind Map as you read. This means that when you re-read your Mind Map, the colour coding scheme immediately tells you which content the book's author provides and what's down to you.

Apart from being able to increase your understanding of a text with this technique, you can also save a great deal of time with this economical approach. It's quite likely that you've already achieved your reading aim after step 3 – Preview. You can then lay your book confidently aside and forget the rest.

For Advanced Students: Generating a Mind Map from Different Sources

In the first part of this chapter you learned how to work through a text quickly and assimilate its content. This procedure can be taken further by reading several sources of information on a subject, for example, 'zero-emission houses', and combining it in a Mind Map.

There are a number of ways in which you can proceed:

> ✔ You use a Mind Map into which content from several textual sources is inserted. This procedure is ideal if you read several short textual sources, such as internet pages, on a subject. Figure 12-3 displays this procedure.

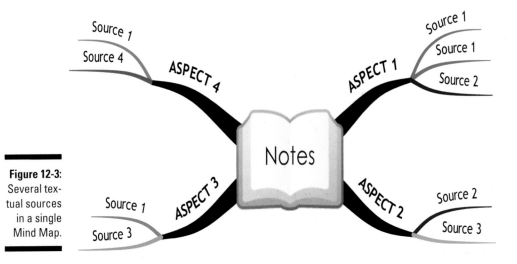

Figure 12-3: Several textual sources in a single Mind Map.

✔ You first create a Mind Map for each text and then generate a final version summarising and combining several Mind Maps. Figure 12-4 illustrates how this works.

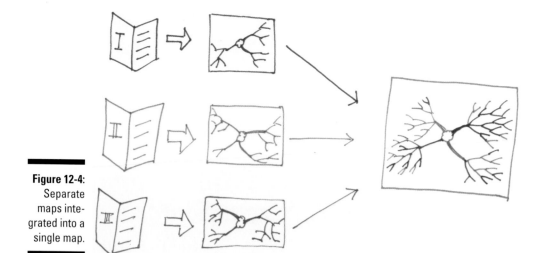

Figure 12-4: Separate maps integrated into a single map.

Chapter 13

Learning and Preparing for Exams with Mind Mapping

In This Chapter

▶ Learning a technique in four steps

▶ Study Mind Maps specially for pupils and students

▶ Further examples

Many books on learning strategies and techniques describe Mind Mapping as a visual learning technique. In fact, generating and structuring Mind Maps can be useful when you prepare for exams too.

Mind Mapping helps here in two ways:

✔ It makes memorising and retaining information easier.

✔ It helps you to understand content and identify connections better.

This is achieved mainly by the graphic form of Mind Maps and the highly individual nature of the technique, involving the use of key words and visual elements.

Preparing for Exams

Many people prepare for examinations by reading books and marking relevant passages with highlighters. Using marker pens does help you to find the relevant places more quickly, but

✔ You must always have the same source material to hand in order to find the information you need.

✔ You haven't processed the source text in your head, as you would by making notes and expressing what you've read in your own words.

Processing material and expressing what you've understood in your own words play a particularly import role in learning and preparing for examinations.

In this chapter I introduce a multi-stage procedure that enables you to prepare for examinations using Mind Maps. It can be applied to books and to classes, lectures or presentations.

The procedure consists of the following steps:

1. Taking your Mind-Mapping notes

2. Entering your own thoughts

3. Revising regularly

4. Explaining your Mind Maps to others

I explain these steps in detail in this section.

Step 1: Taking Mind-Mapping notes

It's quite impossible for your brain to assimilate and retain the content of a book or lecture simply by reading or listening and without taking notes. Learning specialists and educationalists repeatedly emphasise the importance of note-taking. Prof. Stangl of the University of Linz describes note-taking as 'written memory', essential for memorising content. He gives the following tips on taking notes:

✔ Arrange keywords in a non-linear sequence.

✔ Don't write everything down word for word.

✔ Link what you hear to what you already know.

✔ Structure what you've heard.

✔ Develop a system of abbreviations and symbols.

Haven't you heard that somewhere before? Professor Stangl doesn't actually suggest making Mind Maps. However, the aspects mentioned by him are all contained within the Mind-Mapping technique.

What this first step means for you the learner is that you should always take notes, whether when reading a book or listening to a lecture. As you'd expect, I recommend that you make these notes with Mind Mapping. Your

Mind Maps can be generated traditionally with a pen and paper or on a computer.

Moreover, the physical act of writing and drawing Mind Maps is a powerful mental support for learning and helps you to memorise and retain information. As a rule, you'll memorise Mind Maps which you have prepared by hand better than ones typed on a keyboard.

Generating special Study Mind Maps

Now suppose that you're a student and want to prepare for a course examination. Every week you've made copious notes and drawn Mind Maps in your lectures and have also noted down the texts you need to read.

In this example you'll have drawn at least two Mind Maps during each week of the course, one in a lecture and another while reading books.

You can now use the written records already in your possession to generate so-called Study Mind Maps, which are actually a further summary of the various Mind-Map records you've already prepared. To generate a Study Mind Map, work through your existing Mind Maps again and from them make a kind of 'distillate' containing the most important information in a way that makes sense to you.

Step 2: Entering your own thoughts

In Chapter 7, I introduced the technique of 'just writing it out'. This means that you interpolate your own associations and thoughts about what you hear or read into your notes, just as you would in a conversation with the author or speaker.

When you read or hear something, it's rarely the case that you know nothing whatsoever about the subject and it's all new to you. On the contrary, at school and university you constantly connect content with material you're already familiar with. It's usually the case that, when listening or reading, a whole host of ideas and associations with similar and different content comes to mind. It's essential to add these thoughts to your Mind Maps.

This has a number of benefits:

- ✔ In this way you create other ways of processing content.
- ✔ You broaden the context with your own comments.

I find it particularly fascinating to return to my thoughts and reread and extend them when revising (see Step 3).

Step 3: Revising regularly

Over a century ago the psychologist Ebbinghaus demonstrated with his 'forgetting curve' that people forget newly learned content within a short time. There's no precise information on just how high the forgetting percentage actually is, but it's clear that people quickly forget things and this happens shortly after learning. This is why researchers into learning emphasise the importance of revision. Both Professor Stangl and John Medina, author of the book *Brainrules*, point out that anything learned should be revised within 24 hours and then at regular intervals. Precisely what 'regular' means, they don't say – presumably not every day, but certainly not once every six months!

Mind Maps save time when revising

Admittedly, you have to spend some time on generating a Mind Map. But then it takes time making any kind of notes, not just Mind Maps.

You'll save a great deal of time if you use Mind Maps for revising things you need to learn. By recording what is, in your view, the most important content in the best way for you, you can quickly recall such content to mind and revise it efficiently. Not having to work through books and texts again saves you a lot of time. The larger and more comprehensive an examination and a subject, the more time you can save.

Peripatetic learning – a special way of revising

One revision technique that's especially useful for exam preparation or whenever you need to revise a lot of material is peripatetic learning.

This combines physical activity in the open air with the revision of study material. All you need for this are the Mind-Map drawings prepared for your exam. In this way you can revise and reconstruct the content of your Mind Map when strolling in the open air.

The pleasant thing about peripatetic learning is that:

- ✔ Activity in (hopefully) fresh air supplies the brain with more oxygen than when you sit at a desk. This means that the old grey matter can work better.

- ✔ You can forget your regular study or working environment – the same boring old school desk or library seat – for a while and associate what's useful with something nice.

Thinking while walking – the ancient Greeks did it!

In ancient Greece the school of philosophy founded by Aristotle was based on the principle of thinking while walking. This school was called Peripatos from the Greek for the 'hall' in which classes took place. Nowadays this school is also known as the Peripatetic School. Tradition relates that they often held their philosophical discussions in small groups while out walking.

Step 4: Explaining it to others

You'll soon know whether you've mastered and understood your study material when you try to explain it to other people. If you can present content simply and lucidly to other people you may assume that you've understood it. If you have difficulty expressing yourself during your explanation, this provides valuable information on precisely where you should focus your attention.

When giving an explanation, use your Mind Mapping notes as you would a script when presenting a talk.

This last step is well suited to study groups and can be combined with Step 3. You can explain material to each other and interpolate other people's content as they present it on peripatetic walks.

Adopt this procedure step by step. First get used to taking notes all the time and adding your own thoughts. Then generate Study Mind Maps of especially important content.

To make regular revision as pleasant as possible, give peripatetic learning a try.

Especially for Students: Generating Study Mind Maps from Different Sources

As a student you often have to read different specialist texts on the same subject. This means that you need to survey the perspectives of several researchers or branches of research and form an overview of them.

In this context too it's helpful to generate a Mind Map that contains different perspectives on a theme and at the same time to indicate which content or perspective comes from which research branch.

Let me give you a specific example: while studying political science, one of the examination topics for my masters degree was 'Empire Theory'. This involved understanding the different theories about how empires arise and evolve. I had to apply this theory to a specific case and explain the example in a written exam.

When preparing for this exam it was helpful to draw up a Study Mind Map which identified and presented similarities and differences.

You can do this with Mind Maps, for example, by

- Marking different theories/authors/branches of research with different colours.
- Marking them with special symbols (see Figure 13-1)
- Using the resources function of the MindManager software package (see Figure 13-2).

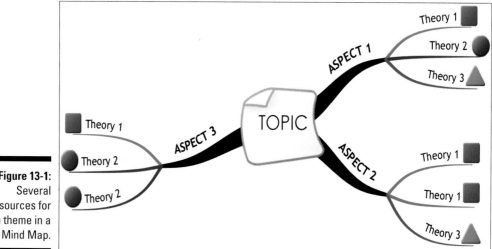

Figure 13-1:
Several sources for a theme in a Mind Map.

Figure 13-2 demonstrates the principle of combining several sources for a theme in a single Mind Map. Symbols indicate which information comes from which source, in this case from which theory. This provides you with an overview of the connections between sources and of details on individual sources.

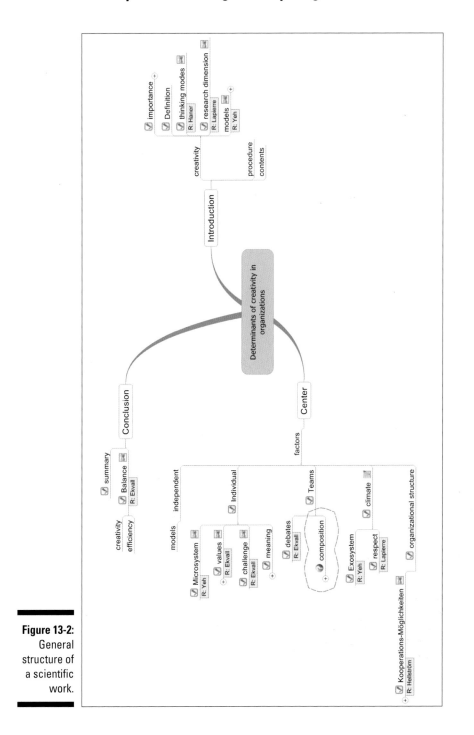

Figure 13-2:
General
structure of
a scientific
work.

Chapter 14

Project Management with Mind Mapping

In This Chapter

▶ Organising projects with Mind Maps

▶ Time and task planning

▶ Generating special views with filters

L ike the word 'innovation', the terms 'project' and 'project management' are used more and more these days. In this chapter I show you that Mind Mapping can also be helpful with project management. Before starting, I first explain what I mean by 'project management' in this context.

There're a number of different ways of interpreting project management:

✔ Project management as the application of knowledge, skills, tools and techniques to project activities or to meet the requirements of projects.

✔ Project management as the control, coordination, guidance and organisation of projects.

✔ Project management viewed from the broader perspective of all management tasks, organisation, techniques and resources for initiating, defining, planning, controlling and concluding projects.

This makes Mind Mapping a tool or technique that can assist you with planning and piloting projects.

'One Page Management': Everything on a Single Page

The book *One Page Management* by Riaz Khadem and Robert Lorber appeared in the USA during the 1980s. In this book, written in the form of a novel, Brian Scott becomes the new CEO of the company X-Corp and tries in vain to gain an overview of his new firm. After a few fruitless attempts he meets 'Infoman', a secretive adviser who introduces the CEO to the art of

One Page Management, firstly in a series of short messages and then in face-to-face meetings. The aim of One Page Management is to obtain an overview of all information relevant to the company in a three-page memo. This memo acts like the gills of a fish and filters out what's essential from the sea of information and saves the CEO from drowning.

Mind Mapping and the way in which the technique is used for project management are rather similar. Mind Mapping enables you to concentrate all the important information you need for the successful management of a project on a single page. Hence, it prevents you from drowning in a sea of project details and helps you to:

- ✔ Survey the project in its entirety.
- ✔ Remain focused on the current stage at all times.
- ✔ Get a better understanding of connections between the different aspects of your project.

Software is Sensible

Naturally you can do project-management Mind Mapping with a pen and paper. An example is given in Figure 14-1. It provides an overview of an online Mind-Mapping course which I prepared. Some of the tips and tricks introduced in this chapter for project management with Mind Mapping can be applied just as well with a pen and paper.

Nevertheless, I recommend using Mind-Mapping software for project management for a number of reasons:

- ✔ **The Mind Map can be easily altered at any time.** In project management you keep having to update frequently changing content. Using a pen and paper for this is very laborious and a Mind Map with many deletions quickly becomes hard to read.

- ✔ **You can convert the Mind Map to other formats.** Most Mind-Mapping programs allow you to convert your Mind Map to other formats, for example, for forwarding to colleagues or for further processing of its content in another program.

- ✔ **Mind-Mapping software offers special project-management functions.** Many programs – in any case the MindManager and iMindMap programs introduced in this book – include special functions for project management that simplify your work.

- ✔ **Software enables you to filter Mind Maps.** Some programs like Mindjet MindManager allow you to filter Mind Maps using criteria of your choice. This can be very helpful for project management, for example, the possibility of filtering individual branches that have special priority or have been assigned to a particular person.

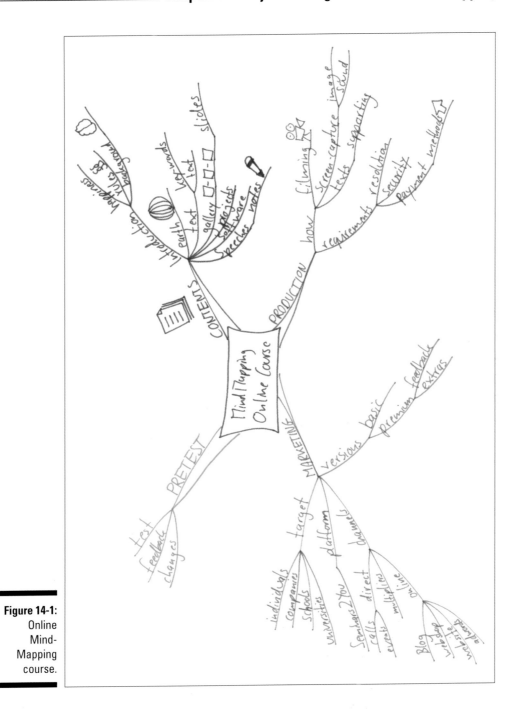

Figure 14-1:
Online
Mind-
Mapping
course.

Projects You Can Plan and Control with Mind Maps

Mind Mapping can be applied to all kinds of projects, be it a summer fete in your garden or designing an aircraft. Nevertheless, there's a small difference between these two examples: designing an aircraft is slightly more complicated than organising your next garden party! Very complex projects may perhaps require other control and planning solutions. There is of course software to help you cope with specialised activities like these.

Nonetheless, Mind Mapping can be sensibly used to manage complex projects, for example, by keeping track of important aspects or visualising individual parts of the project. You've already seen some examples of that in this book.

However, most projects are nowhere near as complex as designing an aircraft. This is the case with both professional and private projects. Mind Mapping and Mind-Mapping software are ideal for projects like these.

Structuring projects with Mind Mapping

Figure 14-2 again displays the online Mind-Mapping course project, at the initial stages of the project, this time using a computer and in somewhat more detail than the pen-and-paper version.

Beneath the main branch 'Production' there is a branch headed 'Scenario' that's linked to an Excel document. This contains a timeline of filming for the online course. The timetable is better presented in tabular form than in a Mind Map.

With Mind-Mapping software you can integrate any documents relevant to your project into your Mind Map.

Additional details with symbols and colour codes

There are now special colour codes and symbols designed specially for project management.

If you work in groups with project Mind Maps you should together determine the meanings of colour codes and symbols in advance and possibly include a key to them in your Mind Map.

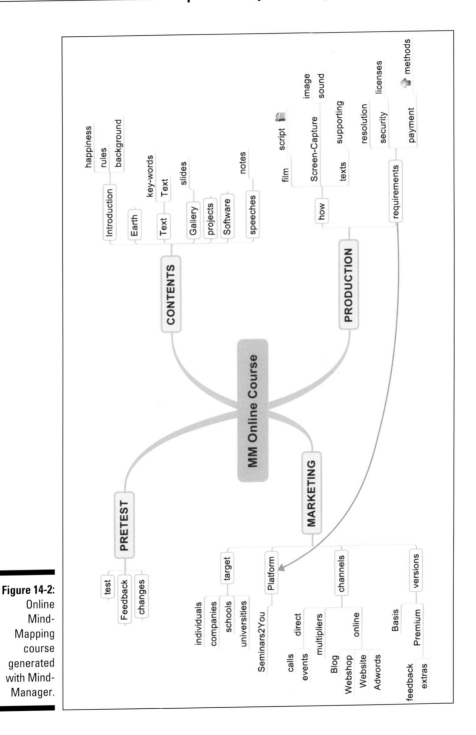

Figure 14-2:
Online
Mind-
Mapping
course
generated
with Mind-
Manager.

In this way you can add additional layers of information to your Mind Map that:

✔ Are eye-catching and easily recognisable

✔ Can be combined with special functions, for example, Mind-Mapping software filter functions.

This principle is illustrated in Figure 14-3. It's based on Figure 14-2 but I've extended it with additional information:

✔ **Symbols with percentage information:** Next to the content concerned is a symbol indicating what percentage of it has been completed.

✔ **Revision instruction:** A red flag next to particular branches indicates that this content needs to be revised.

✔ **Colour coding:** There are two versions of this online Mind-Mapping course, a basic and a premium version. I've marked both these versions on the main branch 'Marketing' with two different colours. These colour codes are also found under the main branch 'Content'. Content which is only available in the premium version has been colour-coded accordingly.

✔ **Resource function:** Mindjet MindManager includes so-called resource functions. These allow you to name the resource proper to a particular branch. I've also assigned resources to the main branch 'Production' and entered the names of people who'll help me to provide course security and include various means of payment in an internet shop.

All the procedures demonstrated so far in this chapter can be done with either a computer or a pen and paper. But software is definitely required for the next few applications.

Time planning and GANTT diagrams

In the chapters on MindManager (Chapter 10) and iMindMap (Chapter 11) I've already shown that both programs are able to display a GANTT diagram with a Mind Map.

Using the online Mind-Mapping course as an example, you can assign a period of time to individual parts of the course . You can display a chronological overview with progress status (see Figure 14-4).

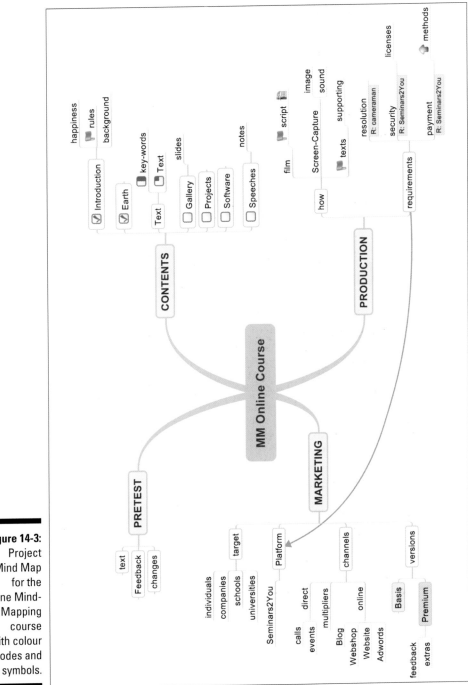

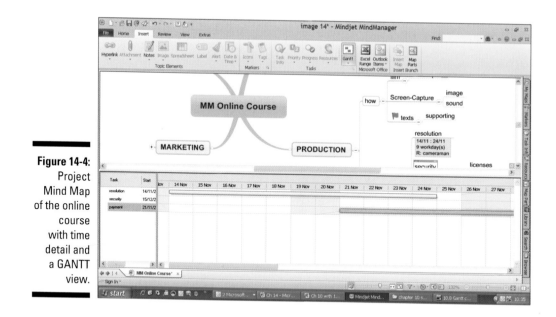

Figure 14-4:
Project
Mind Map
of the online
course
with time
detail and
a GANTT
view.

Filtering special views

If you work with software which allows you to filter, there's a further interesting possibility, namely, generating special views for project management. This is particularly useful for larger and more complex Mind Maps and enables you to obtain a customised view without having to alter the Mind Map.

With the online Mind-Mapping course example, you may want to filter it, for example, to get an idea of:

- ✔ What parts of the project have been completed and what still remains to be done.
- ✔ Which themes still need to be revised.
- ✔ Who is responsible for which areas.
- ✔ Which files relating to the project you've incorporated into your Mind Map.

All this information can be displayed in seconds by using MindManager's power filter function.

I want to filter all those items that still need to be reworked from my draft map for the online Mind-Mapping course. To do this, I highlight in the filter menu the symbol to which I've assigned the meaning 'Revise'. Figure 14-5 displays the result of the filtering procedure.

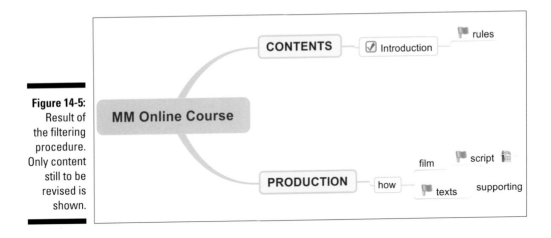

You can use these filter functions:

✔ To provide you with a better summary of the project.

✔ To generate a filtered selection for persons involved in the project, for example, all tasks involving a particular colleague.

Further Examples of Mind Mapping in Project Management

In addition to the example of the online course, I present two further examples of use.

Planning a business trip

Figure 14-6 depicts a business trip that I made to Asia in 2010. I visited six clients in three different places in mainland China and staged seven different training and innovation workshops for them. On each occasion there was a different contact person and different things to arrange like hotel and vehicle reservations. To obtain an overview of which documents I'd already received for which events and to keep track of them all, I prepared this Mind Map. In addition to the main overview there are also links to other documents like schedules and further Mind Maps dealing with individual workshops.

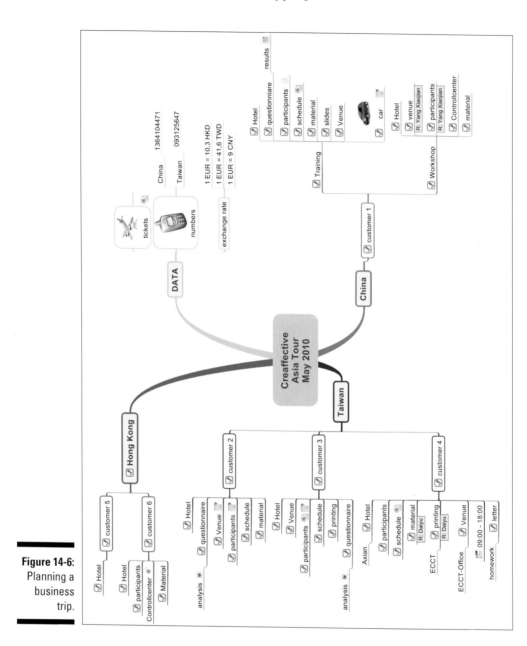

Figure 14-6:
Planning a business trip.

Managing distance learning

Figure 14-7 shows how a Mind Map can be used to manage a two-year masters course. The course is a mix of in-class lectures and online distance learning. The Mind Map helps me to organise my study and ensures that I have instant access to all important information on the course. I'd like to explain a few aspects in brief.

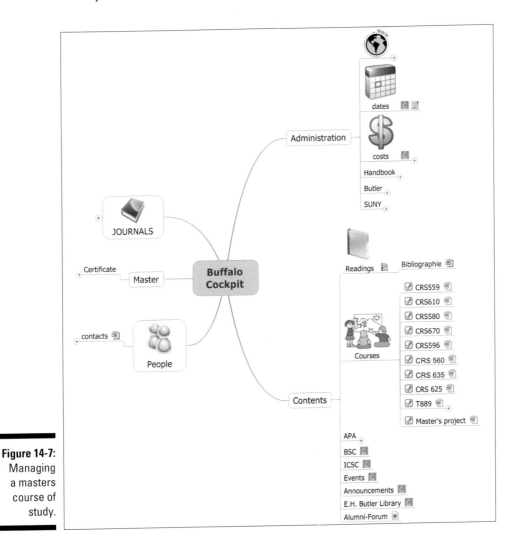

Figure 14-7:
Managing
a masters
course of
study.

The main branch marked 'Administration' contains a variety of information on the course, such as accesses to websites and password-protected forums, plus links to manuals and introductory documentation on the course.

The branch headed 'Contents' is the core of this Mind Map. It contains all the parts of the course I need to complete during the two years. From each course element there's a link to another Mind Map which I use as a project Mind Map for the course element concerned. Further documents and information are in turn incorporated into these sub-Mind Maps.

The branch 'People' refers to contact data of the different classes I've taken on campus and of important contacts in the university's administration.

You can see that there are different ways of using Mind Mapping in project managment. No doubt you too can think of a whole range of small and large projects that can potentially be visualised with Mind Mapping. What are you waiting for?

Chapter 15

Knowledge Management with Mind Mapping

By knowledge management I mean tasks and activities intended to manipulate information in the best possible way. As a method, Mind Mapping can help you with knowledge management in general and especially with personal knowledge management. Mind Mapping is particularly useful for managing personal knowledge, as you can use maps specially tailored to yourself and don't need to worry too much about your Mind Maps being intelligible to other people.

As with project management, you can do Mind Mapping either on a computer or with a pen and paper. I personally work with a combination of software-generated Mind Maps and maps drawn by hand.

Keeping Your Eye on the Ball

A central element of knowledge management is having a clear overview of areas of knowledge and recovering the information you need. As you've already seen in this book, Mind Mapping is useful for presenting the basic structure of a theme in a way that's easily assimilated by the brain.

If you use Mind Maps for knowledge management, you'll design them differently according to whether it's just you who'll use them or your Mind Maps are also intended for other people.

If Mind Maps are to be self-explanatory, that is, intelligible to anyone not involved in their preparation, they may well:

- ✔ Require additional details on sub-branches.

- ✔ Contain additional explanations. You can organise these on a computer, for example in the form of text memos or audio messages.

- ✔ Have more than one word per branch.

The last point in particular is a delicate balancing act. Working with just one word per branch means that Mind Maps:

- ✔ Are very simple.

- ✔ Are clear and don't look overburdened.

- ✔ Can be flexibly extended at any time.

- ✔ Stimulate other associations.

However, this only usually works for the author of a Mind Map, since, when all is said and done, Mind Mapping is an individual technique.

Just who'll be using your Mind Maps, only you or other people too, has to be taken into account when your map is generated.

Assembling Digital Information in a Mind Map

Knowledge management often involves marshalling facts from quite different sources:

- ✔ Facts from a number of different people.

- ✔ Facts stored in very different types of file and assembled in various programs.

Therefore, as with project management, I recommend that you use Mind-Mapping software when applying the technique to knowledge management.

Using software allows you to marshal digital information in a single Mind Map from a number of sources and to access different information sources in a single Mind Map. Another tenet of knowledge management is that information should be accessible as simply as possible. This is assisted by the linking function of software which I present in both chapters on Mind Mapping software (see Chapters 10 and 11).

Example: Personal start centre

Figure 15-1 shows my personal start centre. The figure contains only a small section of the Mind Map, as the whole map would be too large to print on a single page. All the information I need for personal knowledge management is combined in this Mind Map. This means that content which I consider important can be managed in the map. The start centre is similar to the cockpit in an aeroplane, where the pilot has everything he needs to fly the plane immediately to hand.

The branch at the top right displays personal information and the *creaffective* branch contains important content which I need for managing my business. Many of the sub-branches in the start centre Mind Map link to other files containing areas of knowledge.

This means, for example, that with a single click on this start centre I can call up a document I need for preparing innovation workshops, or with two clicks I can recover the content of my course in the USA.

Hence, it's no longer important where the linked files are located on a computer's hard-drive. They can be integrated in a sequence that's relevant to the Mind Map's theme. Furthermore, the source data and folder structure of the hard-drive remain unchanged.

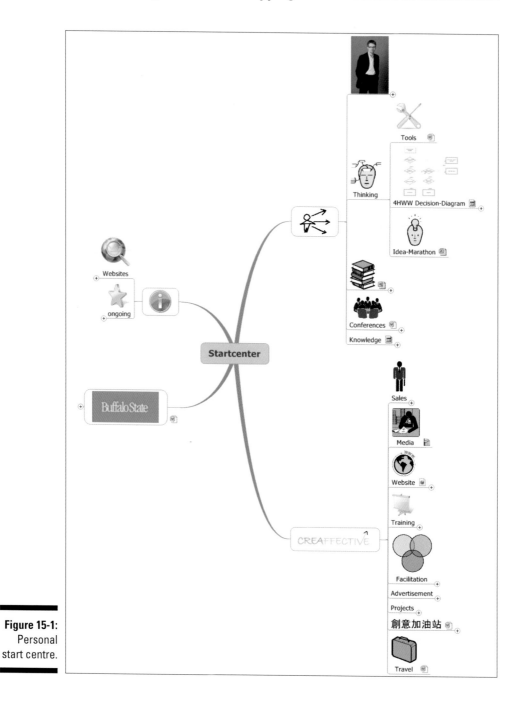

Multi-Level Mind Maps

Every software Mind Map can be linked to further Mind Maps. In this way you can build up an entire knowledge network of Mind Maps all connected to each other. Of course, you can also connect to any other files you choose.

The MindManager software package uses the Multi-Map view facility to display all Mind Maps linked to a MindManager file in a single view. This means that not only directly linked Mind Maps but also Mind Maps linked at a second level are displayed. The principle can be represented as a pyramid (see Figure 15-2): starting from a single Mind Map you can integrate a number of further sources on several levels.

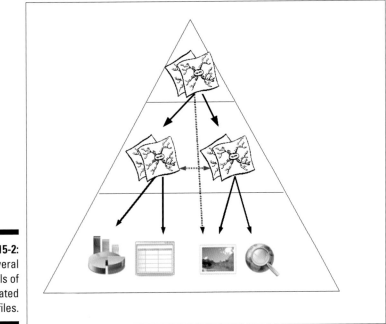

Figure 15-2:
Several
levels of
integrated
files.

Multi-map views in MindManager

To activate MindManager's multi-map viewing function, click on the View symbols bar and then on Multi-map view. This facility provides you with a clear miniature view of all the linked maps of your current Mind Map. This is particularly useful, because the thumbnail images of the Mind Map recall the Mind Map itself to mind, and this is much more helpful than just reading the names of files. When multi-map view mode is activated, a special symbols bar appears.

MindManager's multi-map view function enables you to:

✔ View all linked Mind Maps as a single screenshot in the form of thumbnails

✔ Superimpose several levels of links

✔ Search through all Mind Maps by keyword at the same time

✔ Combine different Mind Maps into a single Mind Map

Thumbnails

When you double-click on a thumbnail in the multi-map screenshot, the relevant map opens and you can work on it accordingly.

This view also lets you know if hyperlinks have stopped working, for example, because a file pathway has changed.

Map levels

The Map levels button allows you not only to display maps linked directly to your Mind Map but also to superimpose links originating in the linked maps.

However, this view is limited only to linked Mind Maps. Other linked files, such as Word or Excel files, don't appear.

Managing scientific work with Mind Maps

Knowledge management is also useful for scientific activities. If you're writing a scientific paper, then you need access to a large number of specialist articles and other sources for quotations to be included in your work.

Mind Mapping can be used profitably here too.

Example: Preparing a scientific paper

Figure 15-3 shows how a scientific paper can be organised (you can see this Mind Map in another context in Chapter 13). For the sake of clarity I present the Mind Map in reduced form. A lot of branches link to my notes on the scientific articles I've consulted for the job. With just one click I can call up the source concerned and work through over 50 different items that have influenced my paper.

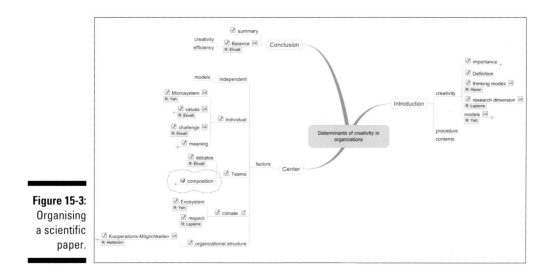

Figure 15-3: Organising a scientific paper.

Example: Displaying Mind Maps in the web browser

A useful way of providing other people with Mind Maps for knowledge management is offered by the website export function of the MindManager software package. Using this, you can export a MindManager file as a clickable image map. This means that a Mind Map is exported as an image file and integrated into an HTML file. The name image file refers to the fact that hyperlinks integrated into the Mind Map can be activated in the web browser.

This makes it possible to display several connected Mind Maps in the web browser and link them together. They can then be passed easily to other people or made accessible on the internet.

Exporting a website with MindManager

This is what you do when you want to generate an image from a Mind Map that can be opened in your web browser.

To do this, click on Webpages in the Export bar.

When you activate the export function, a dialogue window with further settings opens. To export a so-called clickable image map, you first need to select the right template. So, click on the Select template . . . button and select the option Clickable image map as your template under Static organisation.

Now click on Save and MindManager automatically generates an HTML file with integrated images.

Two years' worth of course material in Master Mind Maps

In addition to individual Mind Maps for specific content, so-called Master Mind Maps are generated near the end of the preparation period, displaying all the examinable material in a single map and linking to the individual subjects.

More Ways of Using and Applying Mind Maps

You can see that there are a number of possibilities for using and applying Mind Mapping to knowledge management. Working on a computer provides the greatest flexibility.

You can:

- ✔ Visualise individual areas of knowledge with Mind Maps.
- ✔ Link several areas of knowledge together (for example, when preparing a scientific paper).
- ✔ Manage all your knowledge and facts with Mind Maps (for example, start centre and Research Information System).

Depending on your requirements hitherto and present activities, you can decide what makes the best sense for you.

Chapter 16

Mind Mapping for Creativity

· ·

In This Chapter

▶ Exploring creativity

▶ Using Mind Mapping in the creative process

▶ Brainstorming with MindManager step by step

· ·

Some people like to describe Mind Mapping as a creative technique. In this chapter I argue that Mind Mapping is not such a technique. Nevertheless, Mind Mapping can be used meaningfully in the creative process. To show how this works, I first give you some background about creativity and creative processes.

Defining creativity

Research into creativity has been going on now for at least 50 years. The bad news is that in all this time researchers haven't been able to agree on a generally accepted definition. There are almost as many definitions as there are researchers! However, there are some elements and aspects of creativity that all scientists agree on.

A working definition of creativity which I use runs like this: 'Creativity produces new and useful things.' This definition hardly covers all the aspects I introduce in this chapter but it's useful as a first approximation. Thus, creativity yields what's new and creative outcomes are regarded as useful.

The 4P Creativity Model

All models are wrong by definition, but many can be helpful. One model I find helpful is the 4P creativity model developed by Mel Rhodes (see Figure 16-1).

The four Ps stand for the words 'person', 'process', 'press' (what 'presses' upon a person; the team or organisational climate they work in) and 'product'.

These four aspects of creativity are significantly more comprehensive than my working definition above and describe the most important factors influencing the creativity of individuals and groups.

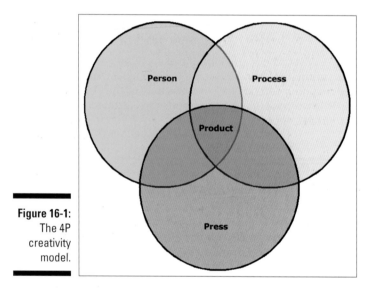

Figure 16-1:
The 4P
creativity
model.

Creativity yields results

An important premise of the above model is that creativity yields a result called a 'product' in the model. This result can be a painting, a theory or a new electrical device. However different these products may appear they represent a concrete result. Hence, creativity is more than just developing original ideas. If ideas aren't used for something then they're worthless.

It's a personal thing

Major elements of creativity are the personal qualities, abilities and skills of individuals. These can be distilled into two upbeat core propositions:

- **Anyone can be creative.** The core message: everyone has the potential to be creative and any mentally sound person can be creative. Except in the case of extremely talented people with special gifts, genes have no role here. The assertion 'I'm not a bit creative' just won't wash.

- **Creativity is something you can practise.** Creativity can be practised and improved. Anyone can improve their creative potential.

The most important personal factors influencing creativity are:

- **Motivation.** Motivation is absolutely essential for being creative in a particular field. If you don't feel like doing something, then you'll find it very hard to produce something new and useful.

- **Using techniques and methods.** Creativity is on the one hand spontaneous and can be favoured by chance. But creativity is in no way limited to this. Creativity is more than just creating the right framework conditions for something. There are many techniques for developing creativity and models for creative problem solving that can help individuals and groups produce new results. These can be learned and practised.

  Mind Mapping is a technique that can be actively deployed in this area and used as a part of a creative process.

- **Knowledge.** On the one hand knowledge is a stumbling block that often impedes creativity. The more you know, the more difficult it can be to think out of the box. But without knowledge, creativity is impossible. If you want to be creative in a particular field then you have to know something about the area concerned.

- **Openness.** Being receptive is essential if you're going to be creative. A creative person can accept new information and ideas without being judgemental about them. This attitude can also be practised and improved by applying a few simple ground rules.

Modelling the creative process

Creativity is not a sudden one-off event that comes out of the blue and favours creative types. Instead, creativity can be seen as a process involving several steps and ending in a creative outcome.

Here too there are a number of models, such as *Creative Problem Solving*. This is a generic model, developed and researched at the International Centre for Studies in Creativity in Buffalo, USA. It can be applied to any challenge in which new ideas for a solution are sought (Figure 16-2).

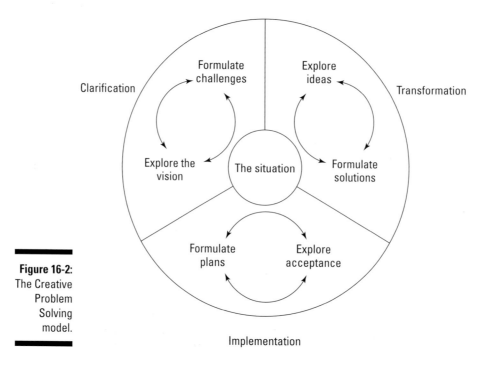

Figure 16-2:
The Creative
Problem
Solving
model.

Each of these models has its own history and its own pluses and minuses. However, what they all do is to perceive creativity as a process that can be broken down crudely into three major parts:

✔ **Clarification.** Before ideas can be developed it's essential to clarify precisely what the issue is that new solutions need to be developed for.

✔ **Transformation.** Once the outlines of the issue have been sketched out, new ideas have to be developed and specific solutions worked out for the problem step by step.

✔ **Implementation.** Once you have the solution, you need to think about implementing it and then actually apply it.

Principles of creativity – two-stage thinking

Whether creativity techniques and processes modelling creativity are used by individuals or groups, there's a crucial principle without which all techniques and processes are useless.

This basic principle involves dividing creative thought into two separate stages:

- **Divergent thinking:** A broad search for many new and different alternatives.
- **Convergent thinking:** A focused, positive evaluation of alternatives.

Maybe you've already met these types of thinking as brainstorming and idea evaluation in another context.

The crucial thing is that both these thought phases occur separately from each other. First you assemble some options and then in a separate step you assess and weed out options to limit them to just a few alternatives. The reason for this division is that we're looking for new solutions and need to abandon old notions.

This is easily said and, in theory, quickly understood. In practice, confusion between divergent and convergent thinking is one of the main reasons why individuals and especially groups are unproductive and unable to develop new solutions, instead returning again and again to old ideas and notions.

Example: Publishing an eye-catching book

Suppose that an author wants to bring out a hardcopy book that stands out from other publications and attracts attention in bookshops.

The question the author asks can be expressed as follows: 'What should an eye-catching book look like?'

At one point in her *divergent thinking* the author develops a range of ideas about how she can achieve this:

1. Make the book particularly large.

2. Make the book particularly small.

3. Produce the book with a shiny cover.

4. Install LEDs in the cover.

5. Use a glossy light-reflecting cover.

6. Use a cover made of stone.

7. Use a cover made of wood.

8. Issue the book in circular form and insert it into a frisbee.

9. Issue the book on newsprint.

10. Publish the book with a towelling cover.

11. Sell the book as a rollable papyrus scroll.

And so on and so forth . . . .

There are now a few options on the table. In the following, separate stage of *convergent thinking*, the author selects those ideas that she wants to examine further and consider particularly promising.

She opts for ideas 8 and 11.

She then has to find out how a book in the form of a disk or papyrus roll can be printed.

One situation you're certainly familiar with is the meeting at which one person makes a suggestion (divergent thinking) and someone else immediately counters with 'yes, but . . .' and explains why such and such an idea won't work (convergent thinking). It shouldn't happen this way but unfortunately this is how it usually is.

Mind Mapping as a Support in the Creative Process

The two stages of creative thinking, as I've outlined them above, are used by both individuals and groups.

Me on my own (no groups)

Nowadays Mind Mapping is often described as a creative technique that helps you to come up with new ideas. A creative technique is characterised by the following properties:

✔ **It tells the user the directions in which she should think.**

For example, there's a creative technique known as the *forced connection* whereby a random image forces the user to make a connection with her problem of the moment. The challenge here is to force a connection between the image and problem concerned.

Returning to our example of the author who wants to publish an eye-catching book: she trawls again through the possibilities and see a glass of water in the context of the 'forced connection' technique. What ideas can now be derived from a glass of water? It occurs to the author that maybe she could wrap the book in a waterproof rubber cover.

So, in this case the 'forced connection' technique involves forcing a connection between the book and a glass of water.

✔ **It's either divergent or convergent – not both at the same time!**

Techniques like brainstorming are purely divergent and compel the user to find new solutions by accumulating a multiplicity of ideas.

On the other hand, there are techniques which can be used to select ideas, that is, by using convergent thinking.

Mind Mapping can't play both roles:

✔ Mind Mapping gives the user no hints as to how and in which direction to think.

✔ Mind Mapping is both divergent and convergent at the same time:

- Applying the keyword rule and using branches promotes the flow of ideas and associations (divergent).

- The action of embedding each branch within a structure and deciding where within the Mind Map structure the branch best belongs is convergent.

If you're on your own and use Mind Mapping to develop ideas, then this won't be much of a problem for you since you only have to debate with yourself about where pieces of information belong.

In a group which has to develop ideas about an issue, using Mind Mapping in the divergent phase of idea development will lead to two things:

✔ The group will discuss where an idea should be placed within the Mind Map (convergent). However, the essential thing about developing ideas is that they initially emerge unstructured and that divergent and convergent thinking should not be confused.

✔ The speed at which ideas are developed is slowed, since when an idea has been developed it has to be fitted into the existing structure.

For this reason I recommend that you don't use Mind Mapping for developing ideas in groups.

Another reason is that in innovation workshops, which I present, a single group can quickly come up with between 100 and 200 ideas on an issue (see Figure 16-3). The sheer number of ideas would overwhelm a Mind Map.

Figure 16-3:
Ideas
developed
in an
innovation
workshop.

Using Mind Mapping in the second stage

Nevertheless, Mind Mapping can be helpful in a creative process, namely, as part of divergent thinking, when ideas have to be sorted and structured. After you've selected from the multiplicity of developed ideas those which you would like to examine further, Mind Mapping can serve you well:

✔ You can now use Mind Mapping to structure and arrange your selected ideas from perspectives that are meaningful to you.

✔ By setting out ideas within a Mind Map you can see which aspects you've covered particularly well and which points have so far generated few ideas and need to be explored further. Structuring ideas may also reveal categories for which you've found no ideas.

Developing and Ordering Ideas with MindManager: A Step-by-Step Approach

One well thought-out method of developing ideas freely and uninhibitedly and then organising them with Mind Maps is provided by the Mindjet MindManager software package and its *brainstorming facility*.

In Chapter 9 I introduced several other software packages with a similar function. The principle is similar for all packages with a brainstorming facility.

In this section I introduce the use of the brainstorming facility for developing, evaluating and organising ideas in a step-by-step approach.

Step 1: Formulating an issue

Figure 16-4 shows a specially formulated issue in the centre of a Mind Map. Imagine that you're a bicycle designer and are looking for ways to improve a bike. The Extras symbols bar contains the option Start Brainstorming. Click on this and an input screen containing three steps appears:

1. Stage 1: Enter all ideas.
2. Stage 2: Initiate group prioritisation.
3. Stage 3: Arrange ideas on group branches.

I won't stick to these three steps here but suggest another procedure.

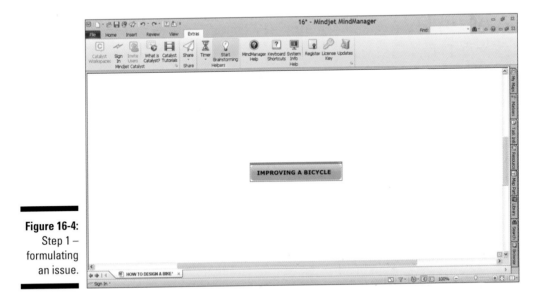

Figure 16-4:
Step 1 –
formulating
an issue.

Step 2: Inputting ideas

In this step you enter all your ideas one after the other in the special input screen. Click on [Enter] and the idea concerned appears in the background of MindManager. At this stage ideas aren't yet assigned to branches but are free-floating (see Figure 16-5).

The one-word rule plays no role in this special use of MindManager for brainstorming. At this stage an idea, especially if it's entered unstructured and visually unconnected with another concept, requires more than one word if it's to make sense later on.

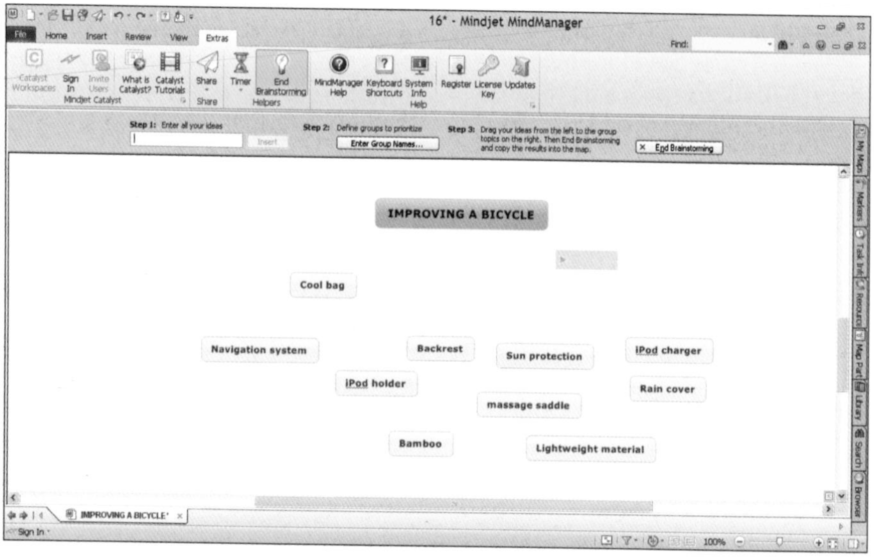

Figure 16-5:
Inputting ideas.

Step 3: Evaluating ideas

Once all the ideas have been entered I exit brainstorming mode. All the ideas remain free-floating in the background of the screen.

When you want to move one of your ideas with the mouse, MindManager tries to add it automatically as a branch to the central idea. However, if you want to initially move the ideas around in the background without anchoring them as branches in a Mind Map, hold down the [Shift] key as you do so.

The main aim of brainstorming (divergent thinking) is to develop a lot of ideas: quantity over quality. Only in the second stage are the most promising ideas extracted from the multiplicity found. This means there'll always be ideas which you have to discard at the evaluation stage. So, instead of going ahead and arranging all the ideas in a Mind-Map structure, you need to sift through them first. This is done by highlighting each idea which you want to retain and attaching a priority symbol to it (see Figure 16-6).

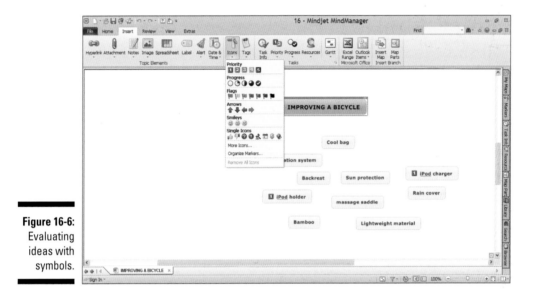

Figure 16-6:
Evaluating
ideas with
symbols.

At the end of this process you'll have highlighted all the ideas to be used at the next stage. But perhaps you don't simply want to discard the ideas that you haven't highlighted?

Instead of just deleting unhighlighted ideas by clicking on each one and pressing the [Remove] button, I recommend that you simply filter out unwanted ideas.

To do this, proceed as follows:

1. Open the MindManager's Power Filter function and blank out all ideas with a priority symbol (see Figure 16-7). After filtering you're left with just those ideas that you don't want.

2. Hit [Ctrl]+[A] to highlight all ideas.

3. Now press [Remove] to delete all highlighted ideas.

4. Then close down the filter. You're left with all ideas with a priority symbol and those you've just filtered out. These are the ideas you'll subsequently look at in greater detail.

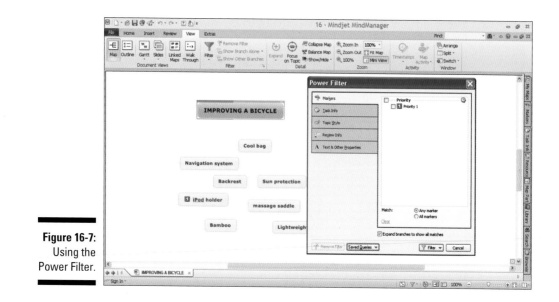

Figure 16-7:
Using the
Power Filter.

At the end of Step 3 you'll have an unstructured mass of ideas that you'd like to investigate further (see Figure 16-8).

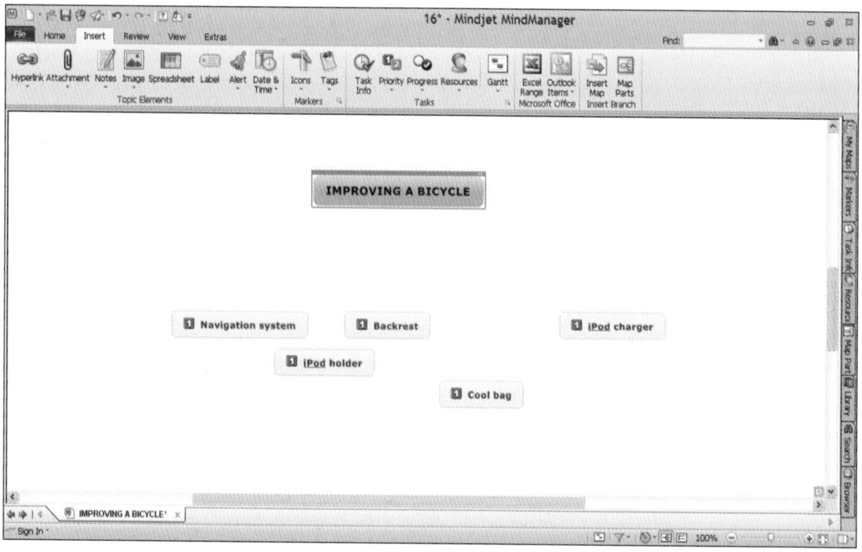

Figure 16-8:
Filtered
ideas.

Step 4: Structuring ideas

You can now use Mind Mapping to start to give structure to the left-over ideas and arrange them according to meaningful criteria.

To make this easier for you I recommend that you first add some main branches to your central idea and call them 'Category 1', 'Category 2', and so on (see Figure 16-9).

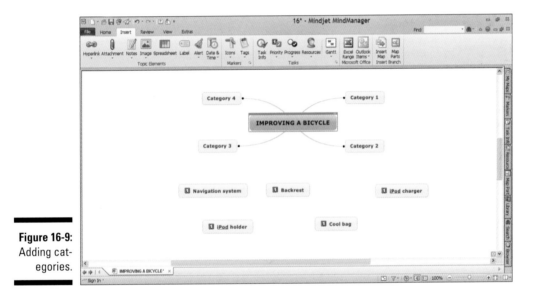

Figure 16-9: Adding categories.

Arrange the ideas from similar standpoints and then give the categories names. You now have a structured overview of selected ideas (see Figure 16-10).

Now you can consider whether there are further ideas you haven't yet thought of for the established categories or whether there are more categories that would make sense here.

As you can see, Mind Mapping can be a creative process as it helps with sorting and structuring ideas. However, as a creative technique for generating ideas, Mind Mapping leaves a lot to be desired.

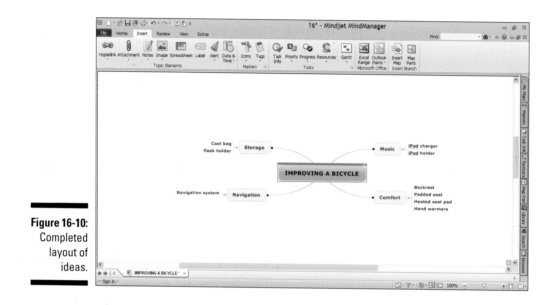

Figure 16-10:
Completed
layout of
ideas.

Part V
The Part of Tens

The 5th Wave   By Rich Tennant

"Before we start this project, I'd like to clarify what metaphors we'll be speaking in. Last time we used sports metaphors. How about using cooking metaphors? 'Half baked,' 'burnt,' 'simmering,' that sort of thing?"

In this part . . .

Every *For Dummies* book includes a Part of Tens section with at least a couple of chapters full of tips and tricks to help you make even better use of the book.

This part suggests tips involving aspects from all the other chapters of the book. You see how Mind Mapping can quickly become an everyday technique and how efficiently you can apply it.

I also refer you to some good articles that you can consult on the subject of Mind Mapping.

Chapter 17

Ten Tips for Working Efficiently with Mind Mapping

In This Chapter

▶ Choosing materials and equipment

▶ Considering the content of Mind Mapping

▶ Using software

Mind Mapping is very easy and yet has many areas of application. So you don't feel overwhelmed by all the possibilities, in this chapter I give you ten tips on how to work quickly and efficiently with Mind Mapping. Some of these tips involve drawing maps traditionally with a pen and paper, others are aimed at software users and others again are general in scope.

Using the Right Paper

It sounds trivial, but using the right paper is really quite important. If you generate your Mind Maps with a pen and paper then be sure you have the right paper for the job.

The paper for your Mind Maps needs to be:

✔ **A single colour and, if possible, white.**

Many people use lined or squared paper so their writing looks neat and tidy. Of course, in Mind Mapping it's very important that your maps should look nice. But, as I've shown elsewhere in this book, Mind Maps can't be squeezed between lines or into squares. Your paper should allow you to develop your Mind Maps freely, according to the theme concerned. Squared or lined paper would spoil the visual impression. Use plain paper if possible.

✔ **At least A4 in size.**

As a Mind Map focusing on a central idea grows outwards, you need enough space to work in. You can't simply write down your content on lines, one beneath the other, as you would when taking notes.

I recommend that you work with paper of at least A4 size and, personally, I prefer to use A3 paper when working in the office or at home. On A4 paper you can develop your central idea on three or four branch levels before you reach the edges of the paper. The problem of space is cited again and again by beginners as one of the difficulties of Mind Mapping. Therefore, especially when starting out, you should allow yourself as much space as possible to draw your Mind Map without restrictions. I particularly recommend that you allow yourself more space when taking notes from a book or text.

However, if you do still encounter problems of space, there are a couple of tricks that can help you:

- You can attach another sheet of paper.

- You can open another branch and connect it to the previous one with an arrow.

- You can draw your branches back in the direction of the central idea, but then of course you won't be able to extend the Mind Map.

✔ **In a landscape position.**

Ensure the paper is in a landscape position (that is, sideways). Doing so increases the space available for your mind map.

Having the Right Equipment Ready

If you generate your Mind Maps on a computer, then your essential equipment is a laptop running Mind-Mapping software. In my experience, there are still many situations where using a computer, iPad or whatever is either impractical or undesirable. Some examples:

✔ **Meetings.** As omnipresent as computers have become in everyday life, I've only rarely seen people take notes on a computer in a meeting. This is probably because there's something inhibiting about an open laptop. Hence, most people still take notes with a pen and paper.

✔ **Reading books.** Here too I often find people prefer to read books between two covers and not on a screen. Many readers prefer to read without a computer at all and not to make notes on a computer when reading.

Whatever your reason for not generating Mind Maps on a computer, you should have the right equipment to hand. This involves relatively simple but very helpful items like:

- ✔ **An A4 clipboard.** You can attach A4 paper to it and make notes at any time – whether in a meeting or on the sofa. It also holds the sheets together and fits into any briefcase.

- ✔ **A set of fine coloured ink pens.** Mind Mapping is a visual technique involving graphic elements and different colours. Fine ink pens (0.4 mm) have turned out to be very useful for everyday work. I personally work with a set of eight different colours, but you can get by with fewer than this. Make sure that the nibs are not more than 0.5 mm thick, otherwise you'll take up too much space with writing and your sheet quickly fills up.

Using the One-Word Rule

I know that I repeat this like a broken record, but in my experience most people find it unfamiliar and even difficult to use: try to work with just one word per branch.

By using one word per branch your Mind Map ends up:

- ✔ Neat and clear
- ✔ Readily extendible at any time
- ✔ Easily memorised and quickly recalled

Admittedly, it doesn't initially seem so obvious that the expression 'good friends' should be divided into one branch 'friends' and a sub-branch 'good'. But this is the only way you can get the most out of the technique. For example, in the case of 'good friends', other concepts like 'old' and 'false' attached to the branch 'friends' only make logical sense when you have one word on the main branch. My many years of experience as a Mind-Mapping user and tutor have taught me that it's almost always possible and sensible to work with just one word.

Working with Symbols

Gradually build up a set of symbols that is helpful for you. They're quick to write down and can be drawn at any time next to a keyword or instead of a keyword on a branch.

Symbols have the following advantages:

- ✔ They are visually stimulating and the first thing you notice when looking at a Mind Map.

- ✔ They enable you to add further information to your Mind Map quickly and easily.

If you generate Mind Maps on your own, which is normally the case, then you don't have to worry whether the symbols are intelligible to other people as well. The important thing is that they should mean something to you. Figure 17-1 contains my numbered set of personal symbols which I've been putting together over the years. I've collected the symbols from computer programs (refer to Figure 3-5) but I also draw them by hand.

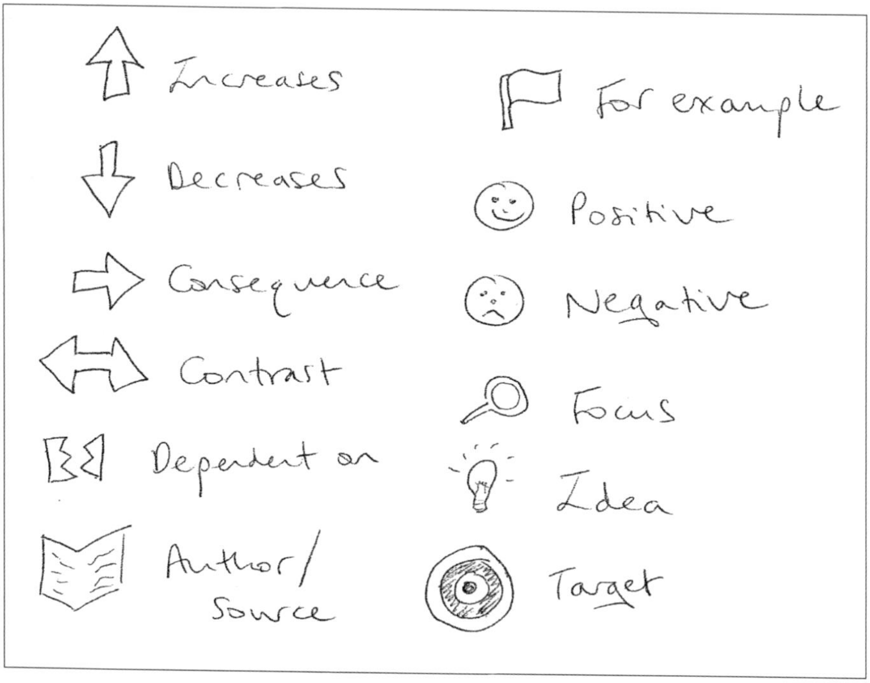

Figure 17-1: My personal set of symbols.

⬆ Increases   🚩 For example

⬇ Decreases   ☺ Positive

➡ Consequence   ☹ Negative

⬅ Contrast   🔍 Focus

Dependent on   💡 Idea

Author/ Source   🎯 Target

Perfection Not Required!

I often find that people are reluctant to develop their Mind Maps further, because they want to avoid revising them or crossing things out. Naturally, this is only a problem for people who draw them with a pen and paper.

Try not to be too fussy when drawing your Mind Maps! If you work with a pen and paper you may have to cross out things or make other changes, especially when taking notes in a meeting. A Mind Map should be a versatile tool – you don't have to produce a work of art or master copy. So, try to get away from the idea that your Mind Map should look immaculate with perfect content. Depending on how important a topic is, you can always produce another version. This 'additional labour' can be an opportunity to rework the theme and structure it better.

Writing in Block Capitals

For the sake of legibility I suggest that you produce a handwritten Mind Map using block capitals. This makes it clearer and a lot easier to read, especially if the branches fan out in all directions. The branches of a Mind Map can criss-cross the page, unlike linear text, which tends to be horizontal. Writing in block capitals definitely makes your map easier to read.

On Paper: Organic Mind Maps

It's increasingly common that people who attend my classes already have some previous experience of Mind-Mapping software. Most programs, like the MindManager software presented in this book, generate Mind Maps in a sort of 'fishbone' layout (see Figure 17-2). In this format the branches are always horizontal and written as if on imaginary lines. This has the advantage of making all the information easier to read.

This form of presentation has a number of consequences:

✔ Because all branches have to be readable horizontally, a main branch must be able to move up or down to make space for sub-branches. This can only be done on a computer.

✔ Having a lot of sub-branches means that the keywords of a main branch are no longer positioned centrally but have to be shifted quite a distance up or down for them to be read horizontally.

The fishbone layout is not what Mind Mapping is all about. In Mind Mapping:

✔ The branches should be free to develop in all directions (see Figure 17-3).

✔ The keywords of main branches should be as close as possible to the central idea.

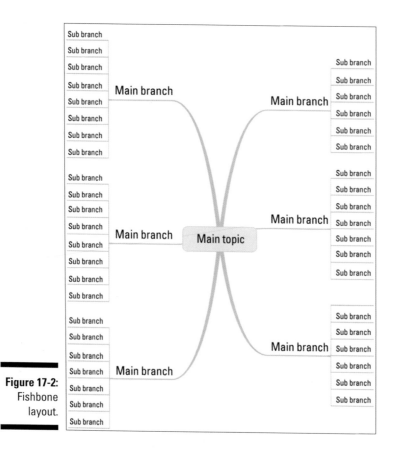

Figure 17-2:
Fishbone
layout.

When generating Mind Maps with a pen and paper, you can't move your main and sub-branches around as you add further information. Therefore, I strongly recommend that you don't use the fishbone layout but design your Mind Map organically. This allows you to extend it flexibly.

Writing in Reading Order

Whether you generate Mind Maps with a pen and paper or with software, there's a natural way of reading maps and for simplicity's sake you should stick to this when drawing them. If you don't wish to number your branches, then start in the one o'clock position, that is, at the top right, and arrange the rest of the branches clockwise around the central idea, as shown in Figure 17-3.

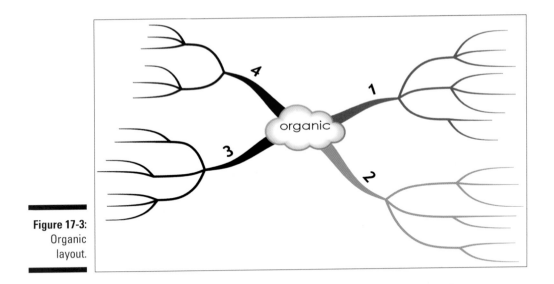

Figure 17-3:
Organic
layout.

In Mind Mapping you don't normally need to number the main branches, since they are read naturally in a clockwise direction. But if you decide to use a different reading order then you can number the branches accordingly. For example, this can be the case when preparing a lecture or taking notes in a meeting – you may decide on a different reading order when you contemplate your completed map.

Developing Mind Maps Outwards and Not Writing Vertically

This tip is useful if you generate Mind Maps with a pen and paper. Now and again I notice in my classes that students draw a main branch at a 90-degree angle vertically above or below the central idea (see Figure 17-4). This isn't wrong but it makes working with Mind Maps more difficult, because you:

- ✔ Then have to write vertically on the branch.
- ✔ Have to rotate the sheet to read it.
- ✔ Find it difficult to extend the Mind Map, because you have to write horizontally again to the right or left.

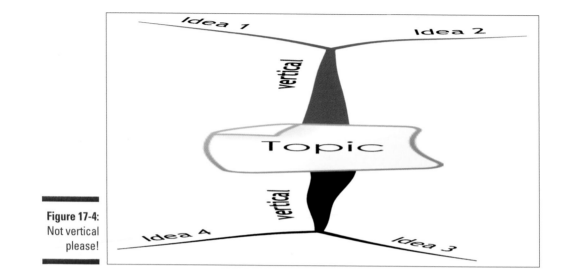

Figure 17-4:
Not vertical
please!

Instead, extend the branches outwards like in Figure 17-3. This always allows you enough space to extend the Mind Map easily and to read everything without having to rotate the page.

Storing Your Mind Maps

On a computer you can always delete branches easily, but this isn't so easy for Mind Maps drawn with a pen and paper, unless you use a pencil and rubber. While you're working you may wish to delete a branch and this is always easier with software.

Furthermore, whilst Mind Mapping, you may need to negate an item by drawing a line through it. You should practise the various ways of differentiating between a negation and an actual deletion or crossing-out.

Filing away hand-drawn Mind Maps

The great thing about software is that you can store your Mind Maps straight onto the computer and have them filed there. With hand-drawn Mind Maps you may end up with a chaotic mass of paper.

As someone who is keen on computers I deal with paper Mind Maps as follows:

- ✔ I put notes on a book in the front of the book itself. So whenever I pick up the book concerned I always have the Mind Map readily to hand.
- ✔ I scan all other maps, for example, notes from meetings, and store them as image files on my computer. I then throw the paper originals away.

In this way you can generate Mind Maps by hand and then file them away digitally and readily access them again.

Generating master copies

Working with Mind-Mapping software allows you to produce master copies, just like with Word and Excel. There are always situations which are quite similar, for example, certain meetings, for which you can store a preprepared template in the memory and the pull it up for further work. Most packages provide you with a few such templates that you can adapt and modify at will.

Using tablet PCs

The middle of 2010 saw the start of the hype about the Apple iPad, an A4-sized device which can be used rather like a smart phone. It means that you can input data directly via a touch-sensitive screen. There's no actual keyboard for entering data, but a virtual keyboard can be superimposed on the display. The Apple iPad or similar devices aren't really suited to inputting large amounts of data, since the virtual keyboard takes up a lot of the screen and entering information is quite slow.

So-called tablet laptops have been around now for over five years. These laptops also have a touch-sensitive screen and can be operated with both the fingers and a special stylus, meaning that you can actually write on the screen. There's also a keyboard for quick data input, and all the programs that run on your PC will work on these machines. They enable you to combine the freedom of pen and paper with the advantages of a computer and are really great for Mind Mapping. In particular, the iMindMap software with the option of drawing Mind Maps freehand becomes a kind of digital paper. You can also write on the screen for the purpose of handwriting recognition.

Chapter 18

(Almost) Ten Tips on How to Make Mind Mapping Your Everyday Working Tool

In This Chapter:

▶ Working quickly with Mind Maps

▶ Tips on using software

*Y*ou now know how to generate Mind Maps and work efficiently with the technique. In this chapter I give you a few tips on how Mind Mapping can quickly become an everyday working tool and be second nature to you.

Practise, Practise and Practise Again!

You can only learn a foreign language if you practise and actually speak it. The best thing, of course, is to stay for a while in the country where the language is spoken, you're exposed to it all the time and you have to use it. People only learn new skills, be it a language, the ability to play a musical instrument or a sport, through constant repetition. Becoming proficient in Mind Mapping takes just a few hours. Here too, you need to practise and actively use the technique, especially at the beginning. You need to apply the technique and practise it when you start learning. Reading this book and theoretically understanding Mind Mapping without doing the exercises and testing what you've read won't help you at all!

Start Small and Take It From There

To make starting out easier and to help you increase your proficiency quickly, I suggest that you get started as soon as possible but begin with simple, clear areas of application.

Don't wait for an application to present itself but actively create situations to put what you've learned into practice within three days of reading this book.

Opportunities for practice might be, for example:

- Arranging a shopping list as a Mind Map
- Putting together a packing list for your next holiday or business trip. You can see my personal packing list for business trips in Figure 18-1
- Taking notes on a longish magazine article
- Taking notes on a TV documentary or while watching the news
- Creating a Mind Map of your 'to do' list (of course in the form of a Mind Map and not a list!)
- Minuting your next meeting with a colleague as a Mind Map

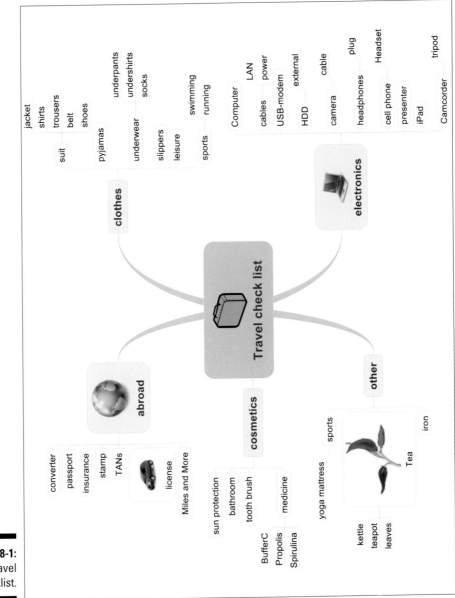

Figure 18-1:
Travel
checklist.

Trying It in Non-Critical Situations

You should get started as soon as possible and practise early on so the technique quickly becomes second nature and you don't have to think consciously about it any more. The aim is to make using Mind Mapping routine. To establish new modes of behaviour and make them routine, it's important that you should feel comfortable and secure. So, when you begin using the technique, choose your situations carefully; these should be situations:

- ✔ With which you are comfortable
- ✔ Where you don't feel under pressure (to succeed)
- ✔ Where you can make mistakes

So I recommend that you don't first use the technique in a very important meeting with a client or in a final exam paper.

Why? In stressful situations people are apt to revert to routine activities with which they feel comfortable. Moreover, in stressful situations the brain is not in learning mode. This means that you switch to behavioural patterns with which you feel more secure and in control. This is when blackouts, which you may have already experienced, tend to occur. What you learned the previous day suddenly eludes you in an examination. This is also because it hasn't yet become fixed in your memory. A doctor who works in emergency admissions told me about the many drills all people working in his department have to do. All employees have to find the work so routine that they can also do it in situations of life and death.

For working with Mind Mapping this means that if you don't yet find the technique routine you revert to traditional lists of notes in stressful situations. Furthermore, you may feel that Mind Mapping hasn't really worked and perhaps 'blacklist' the technique mentally.

Don't Make Mixed Notes

In classes I occasionally see students first trying to produce the content of a Mind Map in list form and then turning it later on into a map. The reason for this is the worry that the Mind Map may not be perfect first time round.

I recommend that you get started with Mind Maps straightaway and don't work with makeshift or mixed forms of the technique. These have never been a success and have the following consequences:

✔ You need more time to create a Mind Map.

✔ You waste a lot of energy converting your list to a Mind Map.

✔ You won't be able to keep track of content.

✔ Your Mind Map itself becomes a hybrid form and looks chaotic and unclear.

Whatever the reasons for writing out content as a list first of all and then generating a Mind Map, I recommend that you start straight off with a Mind Map. Think in terms of 'either/or' and not 'both/and'!

The only situation where you can actually write out a list is when you use Mind Mapping in groups as part of a creative process, as described in Chapter 16. In that case, all the ideas are first written down in unstructured form and the group only generates a Mind Map later as a way of organising content.

Having Materials Always to Hand

Getting Things Done (GTD) is a structured means of increasing your personal work productivity and coping with the ever increasing number of small tasks and interruptions you encounter every day.

There are two important keys to making GTD a success:

✔ Developing the right habits

✔ Having the necessary working materials to hand

One habit you need to get into for GTD is to write down everything that occurs to you immediately in a special notebook. The aim is to free up your mind so you can concentrate on the task in hand.

Hence, the first step is to get used to actually writing everything down. This means that you should have a small notebook with you and within reach at all times. Keep the notebook beside your bed at night, near the shower when you're washing, and in your jacket pocket whenever you go out. If you're not equipped with a notebook you'll never be a good GTD-er!

Something similar is needed for Mind Mapping. To be able to work sensibly with Mind Mapping, you should keep your mapping materials within easy reach at all times.

For example, this could be:

- ✔ An A4 clipboard and a selection of pens
- ✔ A laptop with Mind-Mapping software
- ✔ A simple notebook (A5 or larger) and a pen

Whatever you decide on for your personal equipment, you should keep it with you so you can use the technique at any time. Once you've got into the habit of working like this, you'll find it indispensable.

Making Mind Maps Visually Appealing

You've seen a lot of Mind Maps in this book. An essential thing about working with Mind Maps is that you should find your own maps appealing and so feel like producing more of them and admiring their appearance. This implies the need to develop your own style of Mind Map. The few Mind-Map rules I've introduced give you a great deal of freedom with designing Mind Maps according to your own desires.

Creating visually appealing maps also means using graphic elements. I've argued again and again that it's a good idea to use graphic elements in Mind Mapping. However, you have to strike a balance that's right for you. Many class students use graphic elements very sparingly, whereas others include lots. Here too experience teaches me that adults are not used to working graphically and so it's quite difficult for us at first. Therefore, I recommend that you start out using a lot of graphics to help you get used to them again.

Mind-Mapping software is also useful for producing visually pleasing maps. Most programs generate Mind Maps in a way similar to MindManager software. Again, I've witnessed both extremes in my classes: many people find this style appealing because everything looks neat and tidy and is easy to read. But for others something of the vitality of Mind Mapping is lost. So, please choose Mind-Mapping software that visually suits your style.

Have Fun!

Drawing Mind Maps and shaping them to your individual needs can be a lot of fun. Pleasure in using them is the best starting point you can have. Approach Mind Maps in a playful frame of mind and experiment with the different ways of producing them. The Mind-Mapping rules allow you a lot of latitude here as well. Learning is quickest and best achieved if it's a pleasure and fun to do.

Drawing Maps by Hand and with Software

This too is not an 'either/or' situation. It's sometimes more practical or quicker to draw Mind Maps by hand, but occasionally it makes more sense to use a computer, for example, in project or knowledge management.

Mind Mapping is a way of structuring and visualising thoughts and information. Which method you use, whether a pencil and paper or software, is of secondary importance. To have as much flexibility as possible, I suggest that you work with both methods and decide which is more practical and sensible to use – software or a pen and paper – in the situation concerned.

Choosing Your Software

There's been a real flood of new Mind-Mapping programs in recent years. In Chapter 9 I provide you with some guidance in this area.

It's certainly helpful to try out and test a number of programs at the start, to find the one which best meets your requirements. You should then decide on a package for creating your future Mind Maps. I'm aware of the temptation to try out new software from time to time. However, most packages are not mutually compatible, except as word-processing programs, and you do yourself no favours by having Mind Maps in different file formats on your computer. I work with two programs so speak from bitter experience.

Whetting your appetite with Mind Mapping articles

You're at the end of the book but if you want to read more about Mind Mapping, try these articles:

✔ ThinkBuzan Articles: `www.think buzan.com/uk/articles`. This website is part of the web presence of Tony Buzan, the inventor of the Mind-Mapping technique. ThinkBuzan articles cover special areas of application like Mind Mapping for students or Mind Mapping for teachers.

✔ Wikipedia Article on Mind Mapping: `http://en.wikipedia.org/ wiki/Mind-Map`. The article in Wikipedia is a fairly objective introduction to Mind Mapping without commercial references. The article restricts itself to a basic introduction to Mind Mapping and its areas of application. It also provides references to the literature and websites, if you want to explore the subject further.

(continued)

(continued)

- Also of interest is the comparison between Mind Mapping and the visualisation method offered by Cognitive Maps. Mind Mapping is one of several visualisation techniques, albeit a very powerful and versatile method.

- Biggerplate – Mind-Map Library: `www.biggerplate.com`. A website showing a selection of computer-generated Mind Maps covering business, education and everything else! It contains a library of thousands of examples mainly generated using computer software (Mindjet MindManager, MindGenius, iMind Map5, Xmind).

- Fuzz2Buzz – MindExchange: `www.fuzz2buzz.com/en/mindexchange/browse-grid`. fuzz2buzz.com is a community platform for creativity and learning aimed at bringing together people interested in creativity, innovation and learning techniques from all over the world. One area of fuzz2buzz is 'MindExchange', a forum where people can share Mind Maps, thought techniques and tips on better learning. The site contains many examples of both hand-drawn and iMindMap-generated Mind Maps.

- Mind-Mapping Software Blog: `http://mindmappingsoftwareblog.com`. Chuck Frey with his Mind-Mapping software blog is the site to turn to for new developments in the Mind-Mapping software market. Although the majority of articles focus on software, he also includes articles about areas in which Mind Mapping can be applied generally, most of them involving software.

Index

Notes

Notes

Notes

Notes

FOR DUMMIES®

Making Everything Easier!™

UK editions

BUSINESS

Bookkeeping FOR DUMMIES
978-0-470-97626-5

Leadership FOR DUMMIES
978-0-470-97211-3

Project Management FOR DUMMIES
978-0-470-71119-4

REFERENCE

British Politics FOR DUMMIES
978-0-470-68637-9

DIY FOR DUMMIES
978-0-470-97450-6

Researching Your Family History Online FOR DUMMIES
978-0-470-74535-9

HOBBIES

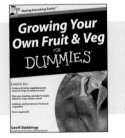

Growing Your Own Fruit & Veg FOR DUMMIES
978-0-470-69960-7

Allotment Gardening FOR DUMMIES
978-0-470-68641-6

Electronics FOR DUMMIES
978-0-470-68178-7

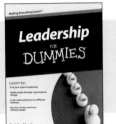

Asperger's Syndrome For Dummies
978-0-470-66087-4

Boosting Self-Esteem For Dummies
978-0-470-74193-1

British Sign Language
For Dummies
978-0-470-69477-0

Coaching with NLP For Dummies
978-0-470-97226-7

Cricket For Dummies
978-0-470-03454-5

Diabetes For Dummies, 3rd Edition
978-0-470-97711-8

English Grammar For Dummies
978-0-470-05752-0

Flirting For Dummies
978-0-470-74259-4

Football For Dummies
978-0-470-68837-3

IBS For Dummies
978-0-470-51737-6

Improving Your Relationship
For Dummies
978-0-470-68472-6

Lean Six Sigma For Dummies
978-0-470-75626-3

Life Coaching For Dummies,
2nd Edition
978-0-470-66554-1

Management For Dummies,
2nd Edition
978-0-470-97769-9

Nutrition For Dummies, 2nd Edition
978-0-470-97276-2

Available wherever books are sold. For more information or to order direct go to www.wiley.com or call +44 (0) 1243 843291

30093 (p1)

FOR DUMMIES®

A world of resources to help you grow

UK editions

SELF–HELP

978-0-470-66541-1

978-0-470-66543-5

978-0-470-66086-7

Origami Kit For Dummies
978-0-470-75857-1

Overcoming Depression For Dummies
978-0-470-69430-5

Positive Psychology For Dummies
978-0-470-72136-0

PRINCE2 For Dummies, 2009 Edition
978-0-470-71025-8

Psychometric Tests For Dummies
978-0-470-75366-8

Reading the Financial Pages
For Dummies
978-0-470-71432-4

Rugby Union For Dummies, 3rd Edition
978-1-119-99092-5

Sage 50 Accounts For Dummies
978-0-470-71558-1

STUDENTS

978-0-470-68820-5

978-0-470-74711-7

978-1-119-99134-2

Self-Hypnosis For Dummies
978-0-470-66073-7

Starting a Business For Dummies,
2nd Edition
978-0-470-51806-9

Study Skills For Dummies
978-0-470-74047-7

Teaching English as a Foreign Language
For Dummies
978-0-470-74576-2

Time Management For Dummies
978-0-470-77765-7

Training Your Brain For Dummies
978-0-470-97449-0

Work-Life Balance For Dummies
978-0-470-71380-8

Writing a Dissertation For Dummies
978-0-470-74270-9

HISTORY

978-0-470-68792-5

978-0-470-74783-4

978-0-470-97819-1

30093 (p2)

FOR DUMMIES®

The easy way to get more done and have more fun

LANGUAGES

978-0-470-68815-1
UK Edition

978-1-118-00464-7

978-0-470-90101-4

MUSIC

978-0-470-97799-6
UK Edition

978-0-470-66603-6
Lay-flat, UK Edition

978-0-470-66372-1
UK Edition

SCIENCE & MATHS

978-0-470-59875-7

978-0-470-55964-2

978-0-470-55174-5

Art For Dummies
978-0-7645-5104-8

Bass Guitar For Dummies, 2nd
Edition
978-0-470-53961-3

Criminology For Dummies
978-0-470-39696-4

Currency Trading For Dummies
978-0-470-12763-6

Drawing For Dummies, 2nd Edition
978-0-470-61842-4

Forensics For Dummies
978-0-7645-5580-0

Guitar For Dummies, 2nd Edition
978-0-7645-9904-0

Index Investing For Dummies
978-0-470-29406-2

Knitting For Dummies, 2nd Edition
978-0-470-28747-7

Music Theory For Dummies
978-0-7645-7838-0

Piano For Dummies, 2nd Edition
978-0-470-49644-2

Physics For Dummies, 2nd Edition
978-0-470-90324-7

Schizophrenia For Dummies
978-0-470-25927-6

Sex For Dummies, 3rd Edition
978-0-470-04523-7

Sherlock Holmes For Dummies
978-0-470-48444-9

Solar Power Your Home
For Dummies, 2nd Edition
978-0-470-59678-4

The Koran For Dummies
978-0-7645-5581-7

Available wherever books are sold. For more information or to order direct go to www.wiley.com or call +44 (0) 1243 843291

30093 (p3)

FOR DUMMIES®

Helping you expand your horizons and achieve your potential

COMPUTER BASICS

978-0-470-57829-2

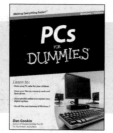

978-0-470-46542-4

978-0-470-49743-2

DIGITAL PHOTOGRAPHY

978-0-470-25074-7   978-0-470-76878-5   978-0-470-59591-6

MICROSOFT OFFICE 2010

978-0-470-48998-7

978-0-470-58302-9

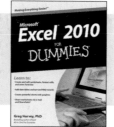

978-0-470-48953-6

Access 2010 For Dummies
978-0-470-49747-0

Android Application Development
For Dummies
978-0-470-77018-4

AutoCAD 2011 For Dummies
978-0-470-59539-8

C++ For Dummies, 6th Edition
978-0-470-31726-6

Computers For Seniors For Dummies,
2nd Edition
978-0-470-53483-0

Dreamweaver CS5 For Dummies
978-0-470-61076-3

Green IT For Dummies
978-0-470-38688-0

iPad All-in-One For Dummies
978-0-470-92867-7

Macs For Dummies, 11th Edition
978-0-470-87868-2

Mac OS X Snow Leopard For Dummies
978-0-470-43543-4

Photoshop CS5 For Dummies
978-0-470-61078-7

Photoshop Elements 9 For Dummies
978-0-470-87872-9

Search Engine Optimization
For Dummies, 4th Edition
978-0-470-88104-0

The Internet For Dummies,
12th Edition
978-0-470-56095-2

Visual Studio 2010 All-In-One
For Dummies
978-0-470-53943-9

Web Analytics For Dummies
978-0-470-09824-0

Word 2010 For Dummies
978-0-470-48772-3

30093 (p4)